THE HEALING CURVE

THE
HEALING
CURVE

A Catalyst to Consciousness

SARA CHETKIN

RAINBOW RIDGE
BOOKS

Cover and Interior design by Frame25 Productions
Cover photograph © SergeyIT and wonderisland c/o Shutterstock.com

Published by:
Rainbow Ridge Books, LLC
140 Rainbow Ridge Road
Faber. Virginia 22938
434-361-1723

Visit the author at:
www.TheHealingCurvebook.com
www.SaraChetkin.com

Library of Congress Cataloging-in-Publication Data applied for.

ISBN 978-1-937907-19-8

10 9 8 7 6 5 4 3 2 1

Printed on acid-free paper in the United States

To my parents for giving me courage
and teaching me that anything is possible.
To Brecht and Adrian for opening my heart and for
turning the endless days into a great adventure.

Acknowledgments

I'd like to thank my husband and my mother for their endless support and willingness to read and re-read every chapter. Bob, my publisher, thank you for your guidance and encouragement in helping me transform what was an academic treatise into a truly personal and revealing story. I'd like to give a very special thank you to Papa; you changed everything. I know you are still with me. And, of course, to all of the healers and teachers I have had the privilege to know, thank you so much. I would not be who I am today without you.

Contents

Introduction

Scoliosis is a lateral curvature of the spine, and depending on the severity of the curve, certain deformities can appear. You've seen elderly people with humped backs. They most likely have scoliosis. My grandmother had it. I have it. Some of the key features are pretty easy to observe. One shoulder is often higher than the other, maybe your head sits a little askew on your neck, one shoulder blade rises up while the other flattens against your back, and your hips are a bit off kilter. These deformities can affect organ function, so doctors usually insist on surgery. They mention scary things like paralysis or problems bearing children. Actually, I'm assuming this is what they do. I've never been to a doctor about my back. Seventeen years ago, when an X-ray revealed a severe curvature in my spine, I vowed to myself that this would in no way change my life. I was fifteen, and I liked my life the way it was. This was bad news, sure, but it wasn't the end of the world. I had my path, and I would continue to tread it, scoliosis or no scoliosis.

With my new resolve firmly in place, I fiercely rejected any tendency of those close to me to treat me differently. I reacted arrogantly to the sorrowful looks of well-meaning practitioners. When my back hurt, I would push harder, never giving myself a rest. I never mentioned back pain. I was absolutely not going to see myself as ill or deformed. There was nothing wrong with me. I was normal. Isn't it funny, though, how so much of what we try to avoid often comes to pass, despite our greatest efforts. I tried my best to dodge stigma because I didn't want to define myself by my condition, but in my obsession with not being defined by scoliosis, I unwittingly created an entire life that is almost solely defined by it.

I have spent an embarrassing amount of time since the age of fifteen considering my back. Either it feels tight or it hurts or I'm feeling guilty that I haven't done yoga yet or that I skipped my Qi Gong practice that morning. Or it feels great and I'm frantically trying to figure out what I did differently to bring about that change. When I go to the grocery store, I choose foods that will keep me as healthy as possible. I don't do this because I want to be healthy for the sake of being healthy. I do it because I want to make sure my body is as balanced and healthy as possible so that it can live with the strain of an already imbalanced spine.

I take herbal baths to ease my back. I buy good mattresses to support my back. I only wear certain clothing to hide the deformity in my back. When my family goes on vacation, it's often to some remote locale to visit a healer who might help my back. Even my spiritual life is wholly directed and supported by this concern for my back. I'm either praying for healing, asking for guidance about how to heal, meditating on the karmic nature of my illness or doing therapy to learn more about how I have created this illness as a learning experience.

When I finally realized how much of my life I was devoting to recovery from scoliosis, I felt terribly cheated. I had wasted my life constantly telling myself that I would eventually be healed, and then I could really live. What I didn't understand was that I had cheated myself. My life was slipping by me, and I was entirely disconnected from it. I was lost in fear and determination, and I couldn't find my way out. I was determined to heal my back, but I was totally at a loss about the rest of my life. I even chose to be an acupuncturist because I wanted to learn about the possibilities of healing from the eastern perspective. It started to look like if I ever did heal my back, I would have nothing left to live for. Scoliosis had propelled my life forward. It was the motivating factor in almost every endeavor.

I saw this as a blessing and a curse. On the one hand, I had to wonder, since nothing seemed to motivate me like scoliosis did, what would I have been without it? I once read that some people have illnesses because without them they would be in danger of living shallow and insignificant lives. At the time, I thought this was a bit harsh. However, once I realized how many things I had done because of this disease, I started thinking maybe the author was right.

I had everything I wanted growing up. My parents ran a successful business and had real estate holdings that provided significant additional income. We had two houses and an apartment in Manhattan. As a teenager, I attended a wonderful boarding school in Connecticut that I loved. It was in an idyllic town, situated on the town green with large trees and lovely houses. In short, it was exactly what you would expect from a New England boarding school for girls. For me, it was perfect. In fact, my parents love to tell the story about the day I went for my interview. We spent the day touring the school, meeting students, and talking to teachers. Everything seemed like a dream to me. As

I walked the hallways I thought about the stories my sister had told me about her time there. I had grown up on those stories, and here I was, about to go through my own experience. As we left the main building I felt exhilarated, anticipating the time I would return; and as we headed for the car I said, "Well, you just lost a daughter for four years."

At that point, I didn't have any problems with my back. We didn't find out I had scoliosis until a year later. To me, my life was unfolding like a fairytale. Life was wonderful and everything was within reach. On top of that, unlike the stories you hear about many wealthy families, my parents were deeply apprecia-tive of what we had, and they made sure that I understood how fortunate we were. They were loving, wise, and spiritual, and I received a good education at home.

However, I still wonder, in spite of my upbringing, if I had been perfectly healthy, would my life have gone in another direc-tion? Maybe I never would have explored spirituality and heal-ing so deeply. I might not have been so interested in half the things I've learned if I hadn't felt the pressing need to explore the possibilities for true healing. This imbalance in my spine has given my life so much purpose. I have searched and searched and searched for meaning. I have delved deeply into myself to understand who and what I am. I have met incredible teachers and healers. I have traveled all over the world from the top of Mt Sinai to the lowlands of New Zealand, all in search of heal-ing and deeper understanding. It has been an amazing journey. I have learned so much, and I believe it never would have hap-pened if it weren't for a rather unruly spine that just didn't want to cooperate.

I call this experience the healing curve because the quest for healing has been a lifelong learning process. I started as a teenager, desperately searching for ways to forget about my condition, but in the process of ignoring my spine, I also ignored myself. I didn't know who I was or what I wanted. Of course, this affected my relationships, but mostly it was my relationship to myself that was ruined. I struggled against my body and everything it was trying to tell me. I shut off my emotions because there was so much fear in me and I just didn't know how to cope with it. I didn't give myself a chance to pursue any of the things I truly cared about. Holding back my emotions translated into holding myself back. I had all of these unfulfilled dreams. Things I was dying to do, but didn't think I could because of my condition. I felt rooted to the spot. Freedom seemed like an impossible achievement for me, and I wanted so badly to feel free. Then, having nowhere else to turn, I started searching within myself. I started looking to my own resources. How could I create a better, fuller life, even with scoliosis as a part of it? I came to accept the idea that I may never fully heal my back. Was I to live my life as a victim? Feeling unfulfilled until my last day? I didn't want to look back on my life with regret. I wanted to learn how to embrace everything, the good and the bad. I wanted to learn how to be happy regardless of the circumstances.

Every experience, even the experience of illness, is an opportunity to deepen our understanding of ourselves and of our world. This increased understanding gives increased peace of mind and creates the possibility for true and lasting healing. We always have the choice to complain about our circumstances, but isn't it more productive to understand how we contribute to them? I think so, but sometimes the answers to that type of question shake the very foundation of our beliefs, and so we don't dare to ask them. This type of question encourages you to know yourself. This type of question demands honesty and self-revelation. The days are filled with crossroads, moments when we can choose to come back to ourselves, to our deepest spiritual longings. At these crossroads we are presented with the choice to develop a truthful relationship to the self or to continue seeking distractions in the outer world.

When I finally had the courage to choose a truthful relationship with myself, I saw just how profound and well-designed this life is. I started the journey seeking a teacher, someone who could tell me what to do and how to reach my goals—I was not experienced enough to think for myself—but as I continued going to class after class and seeking truth in the experiences of others, I started to realize this could only take me so far. The desire to know *myself* grew stronger and stronger until seeking a teacher seemed redundant. I was already my best teacher. The answers that meant the most to me came from within because understanding life starts with understanding self. You are life, living and breathing. You are the meaning of your life. Find out what you are truly made of, and then you will see your health and everything else about you start to change.

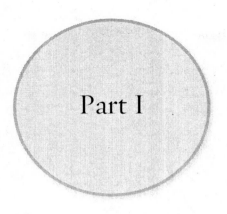

Part I

1

Curvature Revealed

"Ultimately we know deeply that the other side of every fear is freedom."
—Mary Ferguson

WHEN I WAS 15 years old, my back started to hurt. It was a persistent pain, and no matter what I did, it would not go away. I tried heat. I tried cold. I went to the drug store and bought painkillers. I was in dance classes, and I asked my teacher to show me stretches. Even my friends tried to help by massaging it, but nothing seemed to ease the pain for longer than a few hours. Finally, during Thanksgiving break in my sophomore year of high school, I mentioned the problem to my mother.

We were standing in my bedroom at our New York home, and I was unconsciously rubbing my lower back. It had become such a habit, I didn't even know when I was doing it anymore. She saw me rubbing, and asked if my back hurt. I told her that it had been hurting for a few months and wouldn't go away. I couldn't think of any accidents that might have triggered it, and she agreed that such persistent back pain was strange in someone so young.

We decided that the best thing to do would be to go see our family chiropractor, who lived in Key West, where I was born.

A few months later, I found myself sitting in Debbie's chiropractic office awaiting the results of my X-rays. I can still remember the distinct vitamin smell that permeated the entire office. If you've ever stuck your nose into a fresh bottle of whole food-derived multi-vitamins, you know exactly what I'm talking about. It's a clinical smell, but in no way is it sterile. It's fermented, earthy, and alive. That smell is forever sealed in my memory. Even today if I open a bottle of vitamins, the first thing I see is the waiting room in Debbie's old office.

After about a half hour of waiting, Debbie came to the door and motioned for us to come to the treatment rooms in back. The office wasn't overly busy, but I could see people lying on chiropractic tables in the treatment rooms waiting for adjustments. I was feeling vulnerable, and I didn't want anyone to be around when I received the verdict. I walked quickly down the hallway avoiding everyone's eyes and turned to follow Debbie into our treatment room. Then I saw an X-ray on the wall—an X-ray of a twisted, horribly deformed spine. My spine, like a backwards S.

It's difficult to express the range of emotions I was feeling. Another time, years later, I went to visit a close friend who was in the hospital for heart surgery. As I arrived at his room, they were just wheeling him in from the OR, and I remember he looked so weak and so vulnerable. I had never seen anyone my age look like that before. The emotions were so strong that I became incredibly dizzy and nauseous. I leaned against the wall after he passed by me and carefully sunk to the floor. The nurses and doctors walking down the corridor ignored me as I sat there with my head between my knees trying to get a hold of myself. That was a strong emotional response, but standing in the treatment room at Key West Chiropractic, and trying in seconds to come to terms with this new and twisted reality, was pure anguish.

Everything around me seemed to blur until I was simply standing alone, no feeling, no noise, no reaction—just me and this terrifying image that was supposed to be my spine. I knew it was likely that a flood of emotions was speedily making its way to the surface, but I was so paralyzed by fear that I couldn't sense it. I sat down on the treatment table and tried to let this new reality sink in. Suddenly, the other chiropractor that worked in the office stepped in to take a look and let out a little gasp. It was just a small intake of air, but it unraveled everything. What little control I had over myself disappeared, and a deep sense of fear and shame came over me. I felt cornered by that ghastly image, but there was no escape. I wanted to burn the X-ray and pretend that none of it existed. I hated them all for looking so concerned. I hated their clinical discussions about the consequences of such a curve. Angry, frustrated, fearful tears streamed down my face, but I wouldn't let anyone touch me. I felt like a research specimen or a horrific science experiment. I felt ugly, and I felt hopeless.

As I sat there in a daze, my mother began asking hundreds of questions. What would happen to me? Would I end up paralyzed? How would I have babies? What could Debbie do? Should I have surgery? They immediately began working on a treatment plan. Surgery was out of the question. I didn't want it. My mother was completely against an allopathic solution (we don't go to doctors in my family unless death is lurking at the door, and even then it's questionable to us whether it's worth it), and Debbie thought we could avoid it. Instead, I was to fly from Connecticut to Key West every month for treatments. Debbie would just stay on top of it, and as I continued to grow, things would improve. We could halt the progress. They wondered how it had gotten so bad—the worst she'd seen—so quickly, without anyone noticing. My mom blamed it on the fact that I was away at school. Maybe I should come home. I instantly snapped to. "There's no way I'm leaving school!" I cried. "I'm supposed to change my whole life now? Give everything up? Move home? I'm not doing that!"

My mom argued and argued with me, but no matter how afraid I was, I just couldn't imagine leaving my current life entirely behind and adapting this new sickly identity. I didn't want to be "Sara, that girl with scoliosis." I know it's superficial, but next to the fear, the most powerful emotion I had was shame. I was so embarrassed by this whole development that I just wanted to tuck it away. I thought that leading a double life was a better solution. I could go to school and live a normal life, while also focusing on my back when time permitted and when nothing better was on my agenda. My mom was not pleased, but she must have seen how badly I needed to continue on as normally as possible because she relented. Thus began the fifteen-year tug-of-war between my desperate need to be normal and my ardent desire for healing.

I don't know about other people's experiences of disease, but for my part, at fifteen I wasn't prepared to make a lot of sacrifices for my health. I put everything off. I figured I had time later to deal with these issues. To anyone observing me, this might have looked like negligence or disregard, but it wasn't. I was lost in despair. I didn't want to engage in any discussions or plans about my back because I was terrified that one day someone would come with the awful news that there was nothing I could do. Soon I would be paralyzed, unable to have children, and completely alone. So, instead of talking about these feelings, I ran from reality and from the fear and hopelessness I always found there. Even on days when these feelings were like an impenetrable fog, I trained myself to squash them down and ignore them. I didn't want to accept this cruel reality that my life, which had been entirely free from worry just a year before, was now characterized by disease and deformity.

When denial and repression failed me, I would spend the day locked in anxiety. I can remember multiple times curling up on the floor in my bedroom at school, unable to cry or scream, trapped in panic. My friends would try to help me. They would hug me and stroke my hair, trying to mother me back to normalcy, and oftentimes I would put on a good face and get through the day for their sake. Then on other days everything was wonderful, and I would go through the day only marginally aware that scoliosis was an unavoidable fact in my life.

I was obviously not mature enough to handle the emotions I was experiencing. I had never been forced to confront such a serious problem head on. I had never been faced with a painful situation that I couldn't get away from. Scoliosis was like a solid brick wall in my life, a terrifying, unavoidable brick wall. I didn't know what to do about it, and like so many others, I just tried to carry on in spite of the challenges. But always, inside, there was a part of me knocking at the door, waiting to be recognized. The more I tried to ignore it (and I tried really hard to ignore it), the louder the knocking became. It came through anxiety. It came through back pain. It came through shame about the way I looked. It came through all of the little nagging sorrows I felt for myself every day. These negative experiences were calls to action, and they grew louder and louder the more I ignored them. As a teenager, I tried to avoid them by the usual routes: smoking pot with friends, drinking, playing loud music, cloaking myself in various "scenes." I wanted to know myself, but like most people, I went searching in the material world. I was a grunge girl who loved Nirvana (age 15); I was the hippie who loved Phish and the Grateful Dead (age 16–18); I was the feminist into Ani Difranco (age 19–22); I was the socially awkward, creative type listening to Le Savy Fav (age 23–27); I was the yoga-doing, organic-food-eating acupuncturist (age 28–30). I threw myself into these identities completely and totally: clothes, music, hair, vocabulary, and mannerisms. Everything was a reflection of the newest identity, but it didn't work. I was something else, something I couldn't or wouldn't figure out. And that impenetrable, impossible wall called scoliosis was the only thing that could force me to find out just what that was.

When I got bored with the various masks I had been wearing, I started to ask myself some questions: who and what am I? Why do I have scoliosis? Is there a deeper meaning to this condition? How am I contributing to my own suffering? Slowly, scoliosis transformed from a curse cast upon me by an unloving God into a wake-up call created by me, so that I could know myself as an inseparable part of an all-loving God. This transformation has involved every aspect of my life, not just the physical. Healing is a holistic journey. Everything is connected; we cannot compartmentalize our lives. Every experience flows together to create a single picture. Like all of us, my story is an ensemble of highs and lows, a mish-mash of good times and bad, and they all contributed to a deeper understanding of and a more profound and loving relationship to myself, my spine, and my life.

2

A Note on Humility

"True love is a process of humility... When we are
humble we have nothing to fear, nothing to lose."
—Thich Nhat Hanh

TO KNOW THYSELF, SOMETHING I believe to be central to all healing, requires a great deal of humility. I never had much humility as a child; anyway, that's what my family tells me. I'm the youngest of seven by twelve years, so they witnessed my youth in its entirety. I apparently went through a phase of refusing to drink out of anything other than genuine crystal glasses. In my defense, I am certain that this is only because I thought the glass was fun and pretty, not because I perceived its monetary value. I'm also told that at the ripe old age of four, I haughtily challenged my now sister-in-law to a game of chess, and when she informed me that she did not know how to play, I very proudly stated that I could easily teach her. Somehow, learning chess from an imperious four-year-old did not suit her just at that moment, and she refused. I don't blame her. Others were more taken in by my charms, and I have heard that my Montessori schoolteacher was almost in tears the day I finally condescended to let her touch me.

Humility is not an easy lesson for the arrogant, but there is very little one can do to avoid the many lessons of life. It's also true, however, that when the lessons come, we may not always be so eager to accept them. There are, in fact, many things one can do to staunchly avoid the growth that should accompany the lesson. We can, for example, remain willfully ignorant of our part in any circumstance, planting ourselves on the moral high ground and never looking down. We can insist that everyone else is bad, bad, bad and we are pure and loving. What's scary is that oftentimes we can find people to reinforce this belief. If you insist loud enough and persist long enough, people will probably leave you alone, but it only makes the fall harder when it comes. We've all made excuses for our behavior in order to justify the less than gracious parts of our personalities, but through the years I have learned that sometimes it's just easier to own up to your own ugly motives. As they say, one lie begets another, and eventually you are just drowning in excuses, losing touch with yourself and feeling a little ashamed and maybe even a little afraid that someone may find you out. I'm not saying we're all inherently evil. I'm just pointing out that we all have good and bad in us, and there's no sense trying to cover up the bad. Luckily, it has only taken a few small hits here and there for me to get the picture that I am, in fact, not the center of everyone's universe.

A lot of people mention strength and perseverance when they discuss healing. These are important qualities in any endeavor, but I believe that humility and faith are just as important. For example, in my estimation, it takes a good deal of faith to remain open-minded when an aging Brazilian man explains in broken English that he is about to shove a 12" metal stick the width of a large knitting needle into your spine without the use of anesthesia. Or when a portly Maori man with sweet, laughing eyes nonchalantly pulls off the shelf a solid wooden branch with a four-inch diameter and says with amazement that he's never had to use this tool on anyone since it was given to him by a Hawaiian chief ten years prior.

Humility helps us to own our part in any circumstance. It helps us to take responsibility for our lives and to begin making changes where it counts: within ourselves. Yet, I think the most important reason I have devoted so much time to humility is that it takes incredible strength to remain humble, and this intrigues me. In the West, we associate humility with weakness. We're proud of a strong will. We honor a robust personality, and we idolize people who have firm, unwavering convictions. But stubbornness is easy. People are stubborn and arrogant because they are afraid and insecure. Refusing to concede keeps them feeling safe. Humility is more akin to flexibility and acceptance, and it terrifies the hell out of most of us.

I don't know the science behind the mind, body, and spirit connection, but I do know that for whatever reason, the more I mature spiritually, the more my health improves; and part of that maturation is learning about the true nature of humility. It has opened my eyes to something far more beautiful than simply being justified or correct. As I give up my need for control, something far more powerful takes over within me. You can call it grace, you can call it God, the universe, the creator. Whatever you call it, this force is benevolent and omnipotent. It is always seeking harmony and balance. It is always creating joy. When you have the courage to humble yourself enough to experience it, instead of feeling weaker, you feel stronger. Instead of feeling frightened or vulnerable, you feel secure and invincible. I'm not just saying this. I have experienced the shifts that occur when you truly humble yourself.

This has been a very challenging year for my husband and me. We eloped in May to the utter dismay of his mother and family. To them, such a show of independence was completely forbidden, but Brecht and I were on such a cloud from the moment we saw each other, that we didn't want to wait another minute.

We met at Delphi University, a spiritual center in Georgia. I was visiting the son of the director, who is a friend of mine, and Brecht was there taking a class. For ages, everyone at Delphi had been telling me that I needed to meet the handsome and charming Belgian man, who was a new student at the school. I didn't pay much attention to these little cupids, though. I had just gotten out of a rocky relationship, and I was on hiatus indefinitely. I did not want to be with anyone unless they absolutely swept me off my feet. So, when I arrived at Delphi, and my friend Kelly excitedly told me that the Belgian was there, I was really not interested. She coaxed and she coaxed, and I finally agreed to seek him out and introduce myself.

As soon as I agreed, Kelly was on the phone with Katrina, who was cleaning the kitchen at the time. I leaned back in my chair and awaited my instructions.

"Katrina, shhhhh! Is Brecht in the dining hall?"

"Oh. Well, do you know if he is still in the building?"

She smiled at me and covered the receiver "He's still there!"

"Great," I said.

"Are you going to go?"

"I suppose so, but how do I look?"

"Beautiful, of course!"

"Okay, okay, I'm going."

I made my way to the dining hall. It was empty when I arrived, so I sat at a table, pulled my journal from my bag, and started doodling. Eventually a tall, handsome, and disheveled man with wild, wavy hair and a mischievous look in his eye came sauntering in. He was dressed in sweats and a t-shirt, and he looked like he had just woken up from a nap.

I looked up, taking it all in, and asked, "Are you Brecht?"

"Yes, I am," he said, looking a little puzzled.

I stood up to greet him, saying, "Well, I'm Sara. Kelly told me I must come down and introduce myself to you, so here I am."

"Oh! Are *you* Sara?" He looked at me teasingly.

"Yes, I'm Sara . . . what about it? Did Kelly say something?"

"No. I've had several meditations where I hear the name Sara, and I know that's who I'm supposed to be with."

I couldn't help rolling my eyes.

"Uh-huh. Sure you have. Is that what you tell all the girls?"

"Nope. That's completely true. I can show you the entry in my journal." He flopped into a chair at the table and looked at me, smiling and waiting for me to say something else.

I laughed a little uncomfortably and, avoiding a lot of non-sensical babble, confessed that I didn't have a clue what else to say.

His eyes sparkled and he grinned a little too happily. "Well, you came to me! What do you want to know?" He leaned back resting his hands behind his head, and put his feet on the chair in front of him. His feet were huge, and they were the typical man-feet: hairy and frightening, but for some strange reason, I really had the urge to give him a foot rub.

Instead, with a sideways glance and a cocked eyebrow I said, "I hope you're not expecting me to rub those."

"Hmm, it's whatever you're comfortable with." He wiggled his toes in invitation.

"It won't give *me* any comfort! Besides, I don't think we're there yet."

"Really? And what would it take to get us there?" he asked, the grin growing ever wider.

"Oh boy," I chuckled, "you're trouble."

"*Me?* What do you mean?"

"Please, I know trouble when I see it: charming, handsome, just silly enough to be unthreatening. I'm not *that* naïve."

I sat down at the table and crossed my arms in mock defiance. We stared in silence for a moment, sizing each other up.

"Well," he said "since we're sure you aren't in any danger, how about getting dinner together?"

We decided to drive into town. It was obvious already that there was some kind of connection between us. And then on the way to Blue Ridge, he began playing with my hand, holding it, squeezing it, as if we were already together.

"What are you doing?" I asked.

"I don't know; I just feel like playing with your hand. Is that okay?"

I smiled, keeping my eyes on the road and said, "Sure."

At the restaurant we placed our orders and waited in the entryway. Again we were teasing each other, and Brecht playfully put his arms around me. As he did, the feeling of electricity was immediate and undeniable. It was also surprising and unexpected. Sure, we were having a good time flirting, but this was something else. This was a far more powerful connection than a simple flirtation on a Friday evening. We pulled away from each other, timidly avoiding eye contact, and sat on a bench that was in the waiting area. The conversation dwindled into awkward silence, and we stared straight ahead until the food arrived. On the way back to Delphi, the embarrassment passed and our natural compatibility took over. We talked all the way there, all the way through dinner, and into the night. It was 3 A.M. when I finally crawled into bed.

The next morning we said goodbye, and Brecht flew back to Belgium, but not before a slew of text messages and a promise to keep in touch. However, only days after his departure, we decided that a measly one day together was nowhere near enough time, and I was soon on a plane to Belgium. I stayed there for two weeks, but still we hadn't had enough of each other, and a week after I returned to the States, Brecht came to Austin. We packed up my things, drove to my parents' house in Lily Dale for Thanksgiving and didn't spend another night apart for three years.

Six months after that Thanksgiving dinner, we got married in front of a judge in Georgia . It was a sunny day in May when we arrived at the courthouse. The judge led us back to her chambers, which was really just a small room in the back of the assessor's office. She put on her robes, found her Bible and asked if we wanted a ceremony with rings or without rings. "Wow," I thought. "This is one classy wedding!"

"Without rings," we said.

We had known for a while that we wanted to be married, but the actual act of getting married was a spontaneous decision, so the rings came later. The judge flipped through her book of ceremonies, and arrived at the one assigned to ring-less nuptials. She commenced to read aloud what seemed to me a far more religious text than I would expect from a judge. Didn't people go to judges when they wanted a secular ceremony? But this was the Georgia mountains where the simple phrase, "Oh God," was considered swearing. I figured "secular" and "wedding" did not enter the same sentence in this county. So, I remained respectfully quiet. Then I noticed the judge crossing herself and I looked at Brecht, who was also crossing himself. I turned back to the judge, and she looked at me expectantly.

"Umm," I stammered, "is it right to left or left to right?"

"Left to right," said Brecht with a rascally twinkle in his eye.

I gave him a good smirk, performed the holy gesture, and "voila!" . . . we were married! We went home, drank champagne, enjoyed a delicious meal and that was that.

Our little honeymoon was short-lived, unfortunately. When Brecht's family found out that we had married, a round of battles ensued. Our relationship with them had already been unsteady, as his mother was threatened by our closeness and did not like that I was a very independent American. How could he do this to her? What was he thinking? How could he stay with someone like me? Didn't he know I was only with him for money? When it was clear they were not getting anywhere, all communication stopped. For them, it was easier to cut all ties then to allow Brecht his freedom. Although Brecht was extremely hurt by their actions, he knew that he had to cut the cord. It was long overdue. But don't think just because something is long overdue that it's easy. This was not easy, and our relationship suffered a great deal because of it. We might have broken up, but humility is what brought us through.

One night we had a particularly bad fight. I can't remember the specifics anymore, but what it came down to was that Brecht was angry with his mother and because she was not around, I was the only one left to be angry with. Unfortunately, we are both what you might call "fiery"—given over to drama and not at all shy about expressing our outrage. So, we had a fight. A big ol' screaming, yelling, throwing things, stomping around kind of battle. After the storm had passed, Brecht was lying in the guest bedroom and refusing to say anything to me except that he hated me and that I was horrible. And I was feeling pretty much the same way about him.

I was beside myself with anger and sadness. I didn't know what to do. This was not the first fight like this. I knew that he was suffering severely because of his mother's cruelty, but I didn't want to be the scapegoat for that quarrel anymore. I figured I had a lot to think about, and I didn't want to do it in our house, which was cluttered with our things and the memories of the past few dramatic months. Pacing up and down the hallway and trying to figure out what to do, I finally resorted to calling a friend. I began telling her the whole story. She lives nearby, and I asked if I could sleep at her house that night. Her reply helped to change my whole perspective on humility.

She told me to "look up." She said, "Sara, for once during this whole thing, look up. Don't get lost in all of the bullshit. Don't let his mother win. You and Brecht love each other. It's too bad his family doesn't understand that, but you have to live your lives. You know you are always welcome at my house, but first go outside, get on your knees and beg for a miracle. Ask for the grace to get through this." Ten years ago, that advice would have sickened me. But, like I said, I've been learning about humility. So, I did it.

After I hung up, I tiptoed to the back door because I didn't want any questions from Brecht about what I was doing. I came to the railing of the porch and lifted my face to the night sky. With my arms open I asked God or anyone out there stronger than me to help me be in my heart. I asked that love guide my actions, not fear or anger. I asked for support. I asked for a miracle to save Brecht and me from abusing each other further. It wasn't much of a show. I had been crying so much already, I couldn't even muster a tear. Just picture one exhausted woman at the end of a long season of fighting, who, as a last resort, decided to plead to a higher power for the wisdom to change the course of her very new marriage.

It was a cool spring evening, and I gathered my poncho around me and sat down in one of our rocking chairs. I rocked myself quietly back and forth for a while, watching my breath and trying to calm down. I focused on all of the things I wanted for my life. I could see that so much of it was already coming true. If only we could get passed this hurdle with his family, everything would be like a dream. I know all newlyweds say it, but I don't think two people have ever loved each other like Brecht and I love each other. I didn't want to lose that, and I felt like we were at a crossroads.

I stood up and walked back into the house, making a beeline for the guest bedroom.

"Brecht?"

He answered me with a string of profanities, neatly rounded off with a solid, "I'm leaving you."

I sat on the bed and put my hand on his leg. I couldn't believe it, but nothing he said bothered me at all.

I tried again. "Honey, let's make up. I love you."

More profanities.

Again, I wasn't bothered. I know it probably sounds crazy, but, to me, he suddenly looked like a little boy who was lost and scared and in serious need of love. He was no longer the 6'3" 180-lb red-faced monster that I had been exchanging verbal bombs with just an hour before.

Again I said, "I love you so much."

More profanities.

I had to stifle a giggle. I was astounded that no matter what he said, I wasn't bothered. It only made me love him more. I had certainly never experienced anything like this before.

I feel I should mention for the benefit of my female readers, I am not the type to walk away from a fight. I'm more the type to start the fight, if I think there's good reason. I don't back down from defending myself. In fact, I think I tend to be a little too defensive. Yet, here I was feeling so loving and so strong that no matter what Brecht said to me, I didn't care. He may have felt like he was launching grenades, but when they got to me they felt like little feathers just tickling my cheeks and making me giggle. And you know what he did? After about ten minutes, out of nowhere he turned around pulled the blanket up and said, "Oh, just get in bed, get close to me, I need you." And that was the last bad argument we've ever had.

I guess I wanted to share that story because I used to think that being humble meant that you willingly took all of the criticism and emotional garbage people gave to you no matter how much it hurt. But what I've learned is that when you are humble, it doesn't hurt. When humility and love are your supports, there is no such thing as hurt feelings. Only arrogance and pride are hurt by insults. Humility allows you to move graciously through every experience, no matter how "painful." Most important of all, it helps you to confront your demons without judgment. Self-pity and remorse are strangers to humility. Thus, when you have the opportunity to uncover a hidden part of yourself, it is humility that grants you the maturity to carry on in spite of your fears. It is humility that graciously subdues the ego and encourages a loving reconnection to the severed aspects of the self—the parts that we, in our fear and ignorance, cast aside as imperfect and shameful.

Many people don't experience the grace of humility until they are literally on their deathbeds, but I started my lessons in humility a little earlier. When other girls my age were worrying about how to do their makeup or busying themselves building their CD collections, I was coming to terms with a major deformity. I had the decency to recognize that my attitude did affect those around me, and I tried to brush off my feelings so as not to be a total catastrophe haunting the halls of Westover. My downfall, though, was that I thought I was unique. My cross was so big and heavy, what problem could be worse than mine? There were days when I was so angry with my body, I wished I could abandon it on the side of the highway like an unwanted dog or used up cigarettes. On those days, looking in the mirror was like a form of torture. For years, I wallowed in self-pity and bitterness, waiting for someone to rescue me. I became more and more bitter the longer I had to wait for this magical healer to arrive. Until the waiting became unbearable, and I realized no one would be able to help me unless I made some changes in myself, because healing comes from within. And revealing the truth within—even if it's just to yourself—requires a good deal of humility.

I have plunged with much trepidation into the inner void seeking a loving relationship with myself and with my spine. I have striven to forgive my body for carrying this imbalance, and through all of this I have learned that the best thing you can do for yourself is to take responsibility for your feelings and for your life. As soon as I empowered myself in this way, things began to change. At first I would go through small shifts—less pain or more flexibility. Then, my back underwent lasting improvements in appearance. My shoulders evened out, my head rested evenly on my neck. Suddenly, my body started to align itself in spite of the imbalance in my spine; as if the physical part of me was starting to reflect the emotional balance I had been tirelessly cultivating for years.

Be humble. Be willing. Go within. Know thyself! Then healing will happen in a natural and miraculous way.

Healing is revealing.

3

Going Within

"Know Thyself"
—Temple of Apollo, Delphi, Greece

"Whoever knows himself knows well his maker."
—Imam Ali

YEARS AGO, MY MOTHER used to go to a place called Delphi in McCaysville, Georgia and study a healing process called Ro-Hun. At the time, being six years old, I wasn't much interested in what that was, and no one was much interested in trying to explain it to me. But at seventeen the veil was abruptly lifted. Back then, I could have written long, brilliant dissertations about bad luck and the stark cruelty and ugliness of the world, and Ro-Hun, a therapy designed to empower the seeker to move away from such thinking, did not appeal to me. I had absolutely no interest in delving into myself with something like Ro-Hun. I hated anything that smacked of sentimentality or vulnerability. Something as simple as my parents requesting that I sit between them at the theater or on a plane was vexatious and insufferable.

"I'm not a little girl," I'd huff. "You two sit together. I'll sit here."

I could only give my parents hugs when I was coming or going. I could only talk about feelings when I was so over-whelmed there was nothing left to do. I didn't entangle myself with boyfriends or social groups or long-term plans. I wasn't really interested in connecting . . . to anything. You might say that two years of avoiding my spine made avoiding everything else seem natural. So, Ro-Hun sounded like absolute torture. I couldn't imagine willingly engaging in my mom's crazy heart-spelunking therapy—I thought of it that way—just so I could uncover something else to cry about, and in front of a total stranger, no less. But let's just say that my mother can be very persuasive, and one sunny day in June, I found myself lying on a treatment table in mom's office warily regarding Yvonne as she settled in for our session.

Typically, in a Ro-Hun session you lay face-up on a treat-ment table with the therapist seated beside you. After a short relaxation exercise to help you enter into a light hypnotic state, the therapy begins. It's really just talk therapy, but the difference is in the technique. You don't simply tell the therapist what you think about the situations in your life. Instead, when an emo-tion comes, you are encouraged to look for the moment when you first experienced this emotion. From here, the therapist asks questions to help you create a story around this feeling—your story. The goal is to figure out what event precipitated this emo-tion and what thought or belief is connected to it. From this perspective, it is easy for the patient to see how this one belief has influenced countless decisions, and thus the very trajectory of his/her life. It is a simple way to experience personal responsi-bility, that all beings create their own reality. Your thoughts and emotions create your beliefs, and your beliefs create your life.

You make decisions based on your beliefs, don't you? In Ro-Hun you see clearly how many of these beliefs are misconceptions that have contributed to your suffering. These realizations can bring about instantaneous and profound change in people even after only a few sessions.

That day in June, as I lay there in my mother's office, Yvonne instructed me to take a few deep breaths.

"Now as you breathe out one last time, imagine you are floating on a soft, warm cloud. Let your body be fully supported. Just relax . . . ." said Yvonne.

I did as I was told, and at the end of the relaxation meditation, Yvonne asked me to imagine that I was floating three feet above my body.

"Look at your body and know that it is there for you, carrying you through this life."

I tried to follow her instructions, but it was no use. I couldn't bring myself to look. I suddenly felt all twisted up. The more I tried to see straight in front of me, the more I felt as if I were contorted and stretched across the entire room. My left eye was on one side of the room on the floor, my right eye was close to the ceiling in the corner on the other side. I was the equivalent of a giant pretzel. I couldn't see or focus on anything. I told Yvonne what was happening and she told me again to breathe and relax. She mentioned that I was probably feeling nervous and if I would try to relax and not fight the fear, the feeling would lessen. Well, in spite of Yvonne's loving presence—and I mean that, she was and still is today a wonderful therapist—I just couldn't do it. Imagine, if you will, those programs on the computer that twist images from the center, so that everything looks like a spiral. That's what I felt like. My brain was a scrambled mess.

"You don't understand," I said, "I'm . . . I'm all twisted! I can't think straight, I can't see straight. Everything is just twisted."

"It's okay, you're okay. Can you tell me what you are feeling as you experience this?" Yvonne asked.

I told her the truth. I felt nothing. Just frustrated. I had entered the session hoping for some insights about the origin of the curvature in my spine, and I wasn't getting anywhere. We moved on with the session, and as we began to look at other areas of my life, the twisting feeling subsided.

The pretzel phenomena—as I have come to call it—lasted for years. Every Ro-Hun session was a twisting struggle to look at anything pertaining to my body. I simply got used to observing my inner world from that whacky, skewed perspective. The therapists often thought I was just reluctant to share what I was seeing. In reality, my energy was so disordered that I couldn't make enough sense of the images to say anything. Thinking of my spine, it seemed only natural that my energy would be this way. How else could things have gotten so bad? I thought maybe if I could get to the bottom of this twisting, I might have a chance of untwisting my back. It seemed to me that a hidden version of Sara was desperately trying to disentangle itself from another equally elusive version of Sara. The conscious Sara just had to ride it out. It was true on a conscious level already—my whole life was aimed at extricating myself from my spine. But I hoped there was something deeper, a clue to help unravel the mystery. With this in mind, I decided I needed a deeper understanding of the Ro-Hun process. So, I went to study Ro-Hun at Delphi just like my mother had done so many years before.

Delphi University and Spiritual Center is a cluster of houses on the bend of a river near Blue Ridge, Georgia. The river runs along the base of a hill that descends sharply toward the banks, and the houses at Delphi are perched along this densely wooded hillside with multi-leveled decks meandering down to the water. The varied designs of the houses reflect the organic nature in which Delphi developed. First one house, and then another was added to the property, and each has its own distinct character. Arthur Ford is a notorious example. It is feared by some students and favored by those with a taste for adventure. The house is named for a friend of the founder who passed away some time ago. He is said to pay visits to the lucky students sleeping in that dorm. You'll know him by the smell of cigar smoke that fills the room as he enters.

Going to Delphi is like going to another world. Everyone is happy and eager to get to know you. Everyone wants to hear your stories. If they're happy stories, they're happy for you. If they're woeful stories, everyone is loving and sympathetic. It's like a cocoon you can relax in for a while. And like I said, the setting is beautiful. Who wouldn't want to spend a week relaxing by a beautiful river, cozily enjoying home-cooked meals next to a big fireplace and rediscovering yourself day by day?

Of course, when you're actually *studying* the Ro-Hun process, things are a little different. The Ro-Hun students usually arrive in the dining hall pale and tired. They keep to themselves, nibbling on their toast and scribbling in their notebooks. Ro-Hun students are like a giant red flag for anyone thinking of studying Ro-Hun: DON'T! Unless you're *really* ready. Ro-Hun is an excavation process. It unearths and pulverizes all of your flimsy ideas about why your life isn't going your way. It makes you see your part in the story, starkly. You can't avoid it. Don't get me wrong; it's amazing. And it all happens very lovingly, but it's massively transforming. And when you are studying the process in depth, it can get very hairy. You're expected to share your baggage, and you're expected to own it. Frankly, I wish everyone could do it.

On the day of my first Ro-Hun class, I arrived in the Atlanta airport eager to get back to the embracing energy that permeates the Delphi grounds. My Ro-Hun class was small with only seven people in it. That first day we gathered in the classroom at Ro-Hun hall. It's in the walkout basement of one of the buildings that sits near the river. There are cozy couches facing sliding glass doors that lead to the back yard. The funky art on the walls is called Entura art—channeled artwork by Delphi's founder. When I was there, stepping into this classroom was like taking a time-machine to a living room of the eighties. They've since replaced the carpet with wood floors and taken down the neon-colored metal dolphin sculpture.

We assembled ourselves on the couches and looked expectantly at our teacher, Janice. A mischievous smile crept across her face as she welcomed us to our first Ro-Hun session. She gave us a run-down of the process and we discussed the intimidating technique of asking the right questions when the client is teetering on the verge of either a break-through or a meltdown. Then she paired us off.

"Sara, you'll be with Mano."

I looked across the room into the gentle blue eyes of the tall, handsome, well-dressed European man smiling back at me and thought, "Oh, great." I couldn't express my true feelings to hardly anyone, and now I was expected to spill my guts, cry and rant and rave to *him*? I was supposed to reveal my bumbling, snot-covered, tear-streaked face to this fetching European man? Knowing how reticent I was to appear vulnerable in front of strangers and especially men, I didn't think anything would be accomplished that day.

Mano and I made our way up to the treatment rooms. We were in one of my favorites. It looked out over the back yard, towards the river, which you could easily hear rushing by if you opened the windows. The walls were a pale lavender and the sun shone in, giving the room a bright and cheerful feeling. I lay down on the treatment table, and Mano began the guided meditation. All was well until the pretzel phenomena started. At first I just ignored it. I was so used to it, I just expected that it would arrive at some point in every session. But this time I couldn't escape it. Every question led to pretzel. Every answer was unattainable. I didn't know right from left or up from down. Mano might have been talking. I couldn't hear him. I was like the taffy you see getting stretched in the candy store . . . pulled this way and then that way. I was Gumbi in the hands of a four-year-old. I was the most complicated yoga position known to man. And then quite suddenly everything shifted. I was no longer twisted in avoidance. I was totally and completely and very literally paralyzed.

"I'm paralyzed!!" I suddenly shouted. "I'm paralyzed, I can't move!"

Mano jumped up. "What do you mean???"

"I'm paralyzed! I'm in a wheelchair."

"Relax, Sara, take a few breaths. You're not really paralyzed."

Then I saw something that embodied so much of my own fears about scoliosis that I trembled as I looked. A woman with a slender figure and long brown hair was seated before me, most reluctantly, in a wheelchair. She was bitter, powerless, and exhausted from so much struggling. So, this was the image I had spent years twisting myself into a pretzel to avoid? This woman in a wheelchair? Was it me in a past life? *Or in the future?* What was the meaning of this? And why had I tried so hard to avoid it? I did have intense fears about being paralyzed. I thought it was totally irrational until I saw this image lurking in my subconscious. Maybe it *was* a past life, or maybe it was an image I saw in a movie as a child. Maybe it scared me and so I tucked it away. Whatever it was, and that part didn't really matter, it had clearly traumatized me. I was wasting mounds of energy trying to avoid it. I was twisting myself into impossible knots so I didn't have to look.

And no wonder; that image represented everything I felt about my spine: disempowered, cheated, angry, hopeless. I projected all of that onto this one image of a woman in a wheelchair, whoever she was. Now that she was out in the open, those feelings were on the table. I didn't really know it, but until that moment I hadn't dared to feel anything. Truthfully, I didn't even know I was avoiding my feelings. I thought, because of everything I was doing for my spine—like going to Delphi to study Ro-Hun—I was facing the problem head on. On the surface, that was true, but on a deeper level—which is more important— I ran from those feelings faster and faster. But we can run as fast as we like. I've learned that one way or another, everything finds its way to the surface.

I looked at the woman seated before me. She was angry, that much was clear. She was bitter and sad. She felt she didn't deserve her lot in life. She felt hateful and jealous towards "normal" people. And most of all she felt powerless because she was different and she couldn't change that. She was entirely focused on what was wrong, and made no efforts to see anything that was right. She didn't want to look at herself or think about herself or participate in anything joyful or fun. Everything, but especially the idea of joyful things, was a reminder of her belief that she would never be truly joyful. It all pointed to the unfairness and the cruelty of her life.

These feelings were not strange to me. They were me. This woman mirrored my daily experience. Until then, I had been utterly ignorant of my own emotions, but now I could see that I was a mess! I recognized how sad I was and I cried long, heaving sobs. It was a relief to find her, and to face myself. It was a blessing to see a possibility for freedom from these feelings. All I had to do was forgive myself for feeling so disempowered and for carrying this anger and bitterness around for so many years. That was easy when I saw how much suffering I had already been through.

I learned something else that day. There is a difference between facing the truth about how sad or angry or hurt you are and just feeling sorry for yourself. When we feel sorry for ourselves, we aren't confronting anything. We are comparing our situations to others who appear to have it better. The comparison hurts, and we feel bad. The opposite happens when you face your own emotions. No one else matters. Your experience becomes the central theme. You are of the utmost importance. Once you see yourself plainly without the usual masks and excuses, the vulnerability and the fragility of that experience creates healing automatically. Compassion for yourself becomes natural. You joyfully become your own support system, and you realize you don't need anyone else to do it for you. *You can heal yourself.*

I gave the woman in the wheelchair—who was really just a part of me—a big hug and sent her into the light. In Ro-Hun the metaphor of sending someone or something to the light symbolizes a commitment to letting go of an experience and to transcending the belief systems that were created as a result of that experience. She was gone and I was tired. I lay on the table a moment and enjoyed the warmth of the sun shining through the window. I felt calmer than I had ever felt. I wanted that peace to last forever. As I opened my eyes, I smiled at Mano in thanks. I knew that this was a big step in my healing journey.

4

Personal Responsibility

"An eye for eye only ends up making the whole world blind."
—Mahatma Gandhi

Ro-Hun is a process that guides you to self-knowing and personal responsibility. We are all responsible for our experiences of life, but it is difficult to accept this without knowing how you have contributed to the circumstances affecting you. This doesn't mean you can control the situations and the people around you. It means that you are responsible for your experiences of them and your reactions to them. Not only this, but you are attracted to certain situations because they reflect back to you a dynamic that is already occurring within your own personal dialogue. Life is not something that you experience passively. Even the most introverted and shy among us are actively creating their lives. As you take on more responsibility for your life, you begin to see yourself and others in a very different light. Your outlook changes and you begin to make different decisions about how to behave or where to go or what to do. Thus, your life changes.

Sometimes these internal dynamics can seem scary and we want to avoid them completely. But it often happens that if you make a commitment to reveal yourself totally, you will begin to experience them consciously whether you want to or not. In these moments, it is best to just accept the lesson and move on. Otherwise, it's certain that life will continue knocking louder and louder, waiting for your recognition.

Nothing unusual happened the day before the poltergeist. I had dinner with the other students. We had class that evening and then made our way back to the dorms. I prepared for bed and, as I usually do, read for an hour before finally falling asleep. A few hours later, I was wrested from sleep by a loud crash as a pile of clothing and hangers flew from the closet and landed squarely on my head, knocking down the lamp by my bedside. I was so petrified, I couldn't move. I hid under the covers, the clothing piled around me, and tried to get control of my breathing. I wanted to turn the light on, but I didn't dare stick my hand out from the protection of the bed sheet. The minutes crept along. I cursed Delphi for not having "The Clapper." I cursed myself for requesting a single, and then slowly, slowly emerged from under the blankets. Extending my arm to the edge of the bed, I felt around for the fallen lamp. When I came into contact with the smooth, cold porcelain base, I grasped it firmly and replaced it on the bedside table. Thank God the bulb was not broken, and it turned on without a problem. My attackers were spread around me in messy heaps. I suddenly felt the pain in my lower lip as my teeth relaxed their anxious grip. I looked around the room, but there was nothing unusual. I was desperate for a dis-traction, so I started to fold my clothes. When I was finally calm, and the clothing was in a neat pile next to the bed, I turned the light off and hoped for sleep. It didn't take long for the games to begin again. Invisible chimes began crashing violently above my head, and a cackling laugh filled the room. As I was struggling to get to the light for the second time, I distinctly felt someone crawling into the bed with me. That was enough! I bolted up, sprung from the bed, and ran out to the dining room, which is just down the hall. I turned every light on in the place and sunk into a chair. "What the hell?" I said into the big, empty room. The hum of the refrigerator was my only answer. It was still dark outside, but I knew it was nearly dawn, and I was not going back to the crazy room. I turned up the gas fireplace enjoying the warmth, and waited for the others to wake up.

Later that day in my Ro-Hun session, the same energy that had filled the room that night came out of me! I could clearly feel the same chaotic, frightful energy filling the room. It was a great learning: all of the things that are occurring in life are mirrors of what is occurring within. I can be a little stubborn when it comes to acknowledging my behavior and my feelings, and sometimes a gentle whisper doesn't quite grab my attention. I often need a giant wallop on the head (or a giant pile of wayward clothing) to get me to see something. And this was living proof that the dynamics playing within you, get played out right in front of you. Life's great theatre can be a comedy or a big mess. Either way, many of these problems subside if you take an honest look at your own contribution to them. Now, every problem I encounter, I ask myself: what part am I playing to create this situation, and how can I change things for the better?

So, it's clear that Ro-Hun is a wonderful tool, but what if you don't know a Ro-Hun therapist? How do you begin the process of uncovering these fears, doubts, and worries? Luckily, life is so perfectly designed that no matter what you do or where you are, you are always being confronted with your own limiting beliefs.

Consider the idea that everyone around you is a mirror. They reveal to you your own inner dialogue. As you interact with them, observe your reactions. Look for qualities that push a button or make you uncomfortable. These are the keys to unlocking your own secrets. For example, when you have a strong reaction to an individual's behavior, it is certain that this behavior reminds you of your own judgments about yourself. It is impossible to explain this. You must experience it, and to experience it you must have the courage and the honesty to look at yourself without blinders. You cannot soar in this life if you do not uncover your own misgivings, your own faulty perceptions about yourself. These perceptions control your perceptions of your world. It can be no other way. Who you are is what you see. Think about it: you can only truly know something through experience. So, the characteristics you recognize in others, you have already experienced in yourself.

This is good news! Your reactions to every situation in your life provide you with a map to the inner workings of your psyche. When you truly understand this, you do not need to judge or fight against someone because you know as you fight that you are only fighting against yourself. So, instead of trying to change everyone else, allow others their freedom, and you will have the time and energy to rediscover who you really are.

We've all heard the expression, "S/he really pushes my buttons." Have you ever asked yourself where these "buttons" come from? What part of you do people push against to make you angry or annoyed? If you didn't have a particular "button," could they still push it? In other words, if a certain trait no longer irritated you, people wouldn't have the power to annoy you with it. So, why do some traits bother you and others don't? The answer is that the only things that really bother you are those things that hit closest to home; and the personality traits in others that hit closest to home are the traits that reveal to you the aspects of yourself that you are trying so hard to conceal. We all want to be respected and loved, and most of us are afraid, deep down, that we do not deserve the love and respect we crave. So, we try our best to present a perfect image to the world; one we think of as worthy of all the good in the world. We expend a great deal of energy every day creating these guises of perfection. Think of it. It takes far more energy to uphold a lie than it does to just tell the truth. Think of the tension that is associated with telling a lie. Think of the release/relief that comes with telling the truth.

Now, imagine for a moment that all of the things you dislike about yourself took the form of people hidden from the world and from your conscious awareness somewhere inside of you. It is natural that these parts of you would still yearn for expression. (This is not so far from the truth. The soul longs to express itself in all its aspects). Since we don't like these "people" inside of us, a certain amount of energy must be expended daily in an effort to ignore the impulses coming from them. In other words, every day we lie to ourselves and everyone else about who we are and how we feel about it. When someone or something threatens to reveal that lie, we go to battle; and the more energy we are using to conceal that lie, the angrier we will be when it is threatened.

What is the first thing you can do to begin shifting your perspective?

Most of us require a particular set of circumstances to exist before we can conceive of being happy. We have convinced ourselves that to be happy our environment must be a certain way with certain people in it. Otherwise, we're unhappy. In this way, we put our happiness in the hands of others, instead of being the master of our own joy. But your happiness will never come from arranging and controlling your external world. It can only come from your willingness to know yourself fully, and to express joyfully and freely from this knowing. Escape the illusion that control of your environment is the only path to happiness. Reconnect to yourself. Develop compassion for yourself. People are only cruel to each other when they withhold love and compassion for themselves. As you improve your relationship with yourself, you will improve your relationships with everyone else. So, you give the people in your life the greatest gift possible by engaging in this process of self-discovery.

I have found this to be a fun exercise and a good way to develop the skill of recognizing yourself in others. When you are sitting with a group of friends, family, or co-workers, observe each of them and try to recognize an aspect of your own personality. It may surprise you how much your reaction to them shifts when you look at them in this way. I admit, there are certain people in whom I have trouble recognizing myself, but if I persist (even over a period of days) and I ask for that part of me to be revealed, it almost always appears. And the result is uplifting and inspiring! You learn so much about yourself through your environment. The world is truly a perfect gift. The most beautiful thing you could ever receive could not compete with the glorious order and the astounding perfection of the world around you, designed for you to make your return journey—a journey of self-discovery—to your own divine nature.

It is not only your relationships that are affected by your feelings. Our emotions and belief systems influence many aspects of our physical world. Every day you are experiencing your own beliefs played out for you in the world around you because your beliefs create your perceptions and your perceptions create your particular take on the world. From the quality of your interactions to the health of your body, all of it is a result of your beliefs. Your beliefs form your thoughts, and your thoughts create every detail of your life because they affect your choices. However, most of us are unconscious of our thoughts. We are on autopilot, never fully aware of what we are truly thinking, feeling, or believing. We make thousands of choices for reasons we can't understand. We are unconscious. In this regard, my spine has become my barometer. As I delve deeper into myself, I notice improvements in my spine: the healing journey is a journey of self-discovery. You can gain so much from taking a good, honest look at yourself—some call this going within—and seeing who you really are. Understand your own fears and judgments, and your perception of the world will shift drastically, and with that, your whole body will lighten up. If you don't believe it, think about posture or body language. We reveal our feelings in the way we move our bodies and carry ourselves. When we are sad or insecure, we tend to slump a little. When we are feeling confident and proud, we stand straight with our heads held high. This is because your feelings about yourself and the world influence how you create your body every day. That is why it is so important to uncover the roots of your many thoughts and feelings. You could avoid many physical difficulties and improve current health problems drastically just by changing a negative belief about yourself.

I'll give you an example.

I have always had a big fear of being incapacitated through illness—the woman in the wheelchair clearly embodied that fear. She was incapacitated. She felt she had lost her freedom and her chance at a happy life. I have been terrified of the same thing since I was ten. That year my school showed weekly documentaries about the dangers of smoking and the reality of cancer and other illnesses. During the cancer week they showed a *Peanut's* special. The girl had bruises all over her leg, and she didn't know where they had come from. She was also really tired. Then she found out she had cancer. After that, I checked my limbs constantly for bruises. If I found one, it could ruin my whole day. My mom didn't know what to do with me. Often she would just hold me or put me in a warm bath and talk to me, trying to calm me down. To this day, just as I sink into a nice hot bath, my first feeling as I touch the water is a flash of anxiety. Muscle memory, I suppose.

One week, my school showed a documentary about smoking. There were pictures of people who had lost their jaws from cancer of the mouth, their faces all droopy. A few men came to class to talk to us about the dangers of smoking, and they all used those machines that you hold to your throat if your larynx has been removed. Well, I never smoked a single cigarette, and I was terrified of secondhand smoke.

Most of the kids in that class probably weren't so deeply affected by these documentaries. It affected me because I was fertile ground for these fears to take root. Remember, you cannot experience something randomly. You create experiences—no matter how big or small—to teach you about yourself.

Through the years, I felt totally out of control with these fears of illness and nothing seemed to help. I was not at all interested in psychiatric drugs, so my basic solution was just to deal with it and avoid the triggers. This wasn't exactly easy. The three little letters H, I, and V could send me into a panic attack for weeks. "Isn't it a strange coincidence that the *one* magazine I chose had an article about HIV in it? I mean don't you think that's a sign?" I would say to friends or family. It sounds crazy, doesn't it? But our fears appear totally logical when we're in them. I couldn't watch movies about people with MS because I would have to spend the next week unraveling the web of logic I had created that said, "YOU HAVE MS." If I had an allergic reaction on my skin or if anything seemed strange about my body at all, I was convinced it was cancer. It was endless! My life was becoming a maze of avoidance tactics. Only dead-ends could wake me up and get me exploring again.

About six months ago I became terribly anxious, having convinced myself for the billionth time that I was deathly ill. The disease of choice was, of course, HIV. This little virus has been my nemesis since I was in college. I am always scared witless if I start thinking about it. I'm embarrassed to admit how many times I've been tested. Anyway, that night I couldn't sleep because I was so afraid of having AIDS. I went over and over my last relationship: how I made my boyfriend get tested, how he took a long lunch and went to the doctor. He called me when he was trying to find her office. They were doing construction in the building and she had been temporarily moved to another floor. We chatted on the phone as he went up and down stairs trying to figure out where they had moved her. I remember him coming back with the test results a couple weeks later: non-reactive. I remember being very happy and relieved. Now as I lay in bed, I thought, maybe he lied. Maybe he never went to the doctor or maybe he faked the results. He was clever. I mean it's possible. Maybe he already had it and was hiding it from me.

Believe me, this is not the kind of thing you want to be thinking about people. But locked in my fear, that agonizing paralyzing fear, it was all I could think. I had to stop myself from calling him to make sure. Actually, I did that once before with someone else. He and I are no longer friends, understandably.

Fear can ruin your life if you let it.

I woke Brecht up and told him my troubles. He understood and offered some comforting words, but I thought he was being a little cavalier, considering this was life or death. We talked a little while longer, and as he fell asleep I began to do the only thing I could think of to do. I begged the universe or God or whoever to please help me. I lay there on my back, eyes closed, fists clenched, asking for something to take this fear from me. If there is one thing I know for sure, it is that if you truly ask, you will receive. As soon as the words "help me" entered my mind, I was surrounded by brilliant light. My eyes were closed, but I saw light everywhere. Then a hand—yes, a hand—reached into my head, and pulled something out. I don't know what it was, but it felt as if someone had pulled a floppy disk out of my brain. That terribly flimsy explanation is the best I can come up with. The hand pulled a large, glowing floppy disk out of my head, and "poof" I was calm as can be. I tearfully thanked the owner of the hand, rolled over, put my arms around Brecht and fell asleep.

When we woke up the next morning I felt really wonderful, as though I had let go of something big. I realized that my fears were like a computer program I was running over and over again. The message? Change the program. I don't know how other people experience their lives, but for a long time I never felt safe. I never felt totally secure and at ease. I didn't know what would help me to establish the sense of security I was seeking. I meditated all of the time. Every day I did some form of spiritual practice. It never brought me any closer to *lasting* peace. It gave me moments of profound peace. It clarified my perceptions. It showed me where I was tripping up, and I have worked with that. The only thing that truly helps is to reveal, reveal, reveal. The more conscious I am of my own pitfalls, the easier it is to cultivate peacefulness. Anyway, I wouldn't call the spiritual path a walk in the park. It's the complete opposite, actually.

When we woke up the next morning I felt really wonderful, as though I had let go of something big. I know that the battle isn't entirely over. Just writing the beginning of this little blurb has left me teetering on the edge of another fear episode. But I allowed something to happen. Instead of lying awake all night, and then finally falling asleep at dawn, I shifted something and slept peacefully. This was a big improvement.

Brecht got out of bed and headed for the bathroom. I listened to him brushing his teeth and waited for him to say "you don't have to get up!" He always says that, and I know it's silly, but it always bothers me. I know I don't have to get up, but I like to get up. I can't stand the idea that he is downstairs enjoying a delicious cup of coffee, while I'm just wasting time lying in bed. I'm not competitive with most things, but the really stupid things in life, like who gets out of bed first . . . oh, I'm all over that. But he didn't say, "You don't have to get up." He said, "My beautiful wife is still lying in bed. You look so beautiful!" I smiled and brushed the matted hair out of my eyes. He began putting away the clean laundry. It had been sitting in a basket on the floor for days. I got up to help him and sat next to the basket where some shirts had fallen out. As I was folding, I could feel him staring at my back. This always makes me uneasy, so I looked at him and said, "What?"

"I can't believe it, babe. I mean your back, it's so amazing. It looks so much better, I get emotional just looking at it. It's really incredible. Can you see it?"

I stood up and looked in the mirror. It did, indeed, look a lot better than it had the night before. I told him what had happened with the floppy disk, but what do you say to something like that? His reply was, "Wow. Well, you definitely let go of something because your back looks even better today."

I was grateful for the healing I received that night. Yet, it wasn't a lasting solution to these deep-seated fears. I wanted to uncover the root of this belief that I was always in danger of becoming terribly ill. Why did I feel that way? Other than my back, I had hardly been sick a day in my life! And it seemed to me that housing this fear would only attract more imbalance into my body.

A few months later, Brecht and I boarded a plane to London to attend a trance-healing workshop at the Arthur Findlay School in Stansted, England. The school is located at Stansted Hall, a small nineteenth-century estate in the countryside north of London. J. Arthur Findlay, a businessman and spiritualist, donated the hall to the Spiritualist National Union in 1964, after the death of his wife. The house and grounds have been wonderfully kept up, and when you attend the school you feel as if you are being transported back in time. The main hall boasts a grand staircase, soaring ceilings, and an elegant sitting area with beautifully refurbished period furniture, oriental rugs, and a large fireplace. Floor-to-ceiling windows open onto fields and gardens. The classes take place in the rooms adjoining this hall, which is really the center of the house. Our class met in the former library, another impressive feat in restoration and attention to period detail. The woodwork, the bookshelves, the draperies, the windows, all reflected the care that the SNU takes in maintaining this house for the enjoyment of the students.

Not only is the house itself lovingly cared for, but the grounds are also pleasantly manicured. In my opinion, there is no countryside as gentle and welcoming as the English countryside. Brecht and I took many long walks during our time at Stansted. On these excursions, I allowed my imagination to meander through a Jane Austen novel. I was Lizzie walking with Mr. Darcy through their estate. I was Elinor and Marianne Dashwood walking in the countryside around their cottage. The paths were sprinkled with wild flowers, the oak trees were large and imposing. Rabbits ran in and out of the little forest. Horses munched on grass in the fields. The days were warm and the sun was always shining. And I was with my favorite travel companion, studying one of my favorite subjects. Everything was perfect.

Then one day, I started to feel very anxious. As I was walking up the grand staircase to go back to my room, I suddenly became conscious of a hidden desire to be seriously ill. As a confessed hypochondriac, this was really confusing and scary, but I didn't run from it like I often do. I wanted to learn about this desire. Maybe this was the moment when I could finally gain some clarity about all of my fears. I went to my room and sat quietly with my eyes closed. I allowed the desire, along with the fear, to come fully over me as I remained objective and observed the thoughts I was having in relation to this fear. Why did this desire exist? I remembered a previous Ro-Hun session when I discovered the fact that I believed people with illnesses were treated with more compassion, love, and forgiveness. That somehow being ill was a convenient way to avoid judgment and to gain positive attention. It seemed that subconsciously, I had a desire to be ill. And now, somehow, I was able to experience that desire in a fully conscious state.

Could it be that my conscious fear of illness came from my subconscious desire for the forgiveness and unconditional love that I believed was generously lavished upon people who are ill? I realized a certain dynamic had been occurring within me completely under the radar for years: the subconscious desire to be ill—and the subsequent conscious terror at the prospect of being ill. As I came to this realization, I had another breakthrough. The year that I started to have so much fear about illness (at the age of 10) was the same year I decided that illness was a good way to attract love and attention (I learned this in my Ro-Hun session). That clinched it for me. As soon as I saw this dynamic at play, it was easy to understand my fearful attitude. As soon as I understood what was happening, it was much easier to let it go, and I felt a huge surge of joy and uplifting. I was grateful that I had the awareness to listen when this part of me reached out for healing. I felt at one with myself, and since then my fears have subsided almost completely.

We all have subconscious dynamics playing within us, and the fears and misconceptions that arise from these dynamics deeply affect our conscious state of mind. These thoughts and feelings are there for us to uncover, but it takes tremendous work to bring them to the surface for healing. That is, it takes tremendous work unless you're mind is quiet enough, still enough, to recognize a sign when it is receiving one. Your subconscious is always sending you messages, clues to help you unravel the mystery of who you are; but we rarely recognize these signs through the cluttered distractions and compulsive behavior of modern society. An important step in achieving a more intimate relationship with the self is allowing for more quiet in your life. In other words, less TV/movies, fewer trips to the mall, fewer trips to the bar or the club, more meditation or, at least, more time simply sitting quietly. For many of us, trying to pay attention to the communications coming from within is like trying to hear a whisper in the middle of a rock concert—not working! Do anything you can think of to help quiet your environment. The more stillness you create within you and around you, the more likely you are to be receptive to signals that your subconscious, internal environment is sending. From there, healing is easy. Once you see a dynamic at play, you come to a more profound understanding of your behavior. After that, it's only matter of breaking a habit, and you're free. One less compulsion to deal with!

Remember: healing is revealing.

5

Mr. Gedes / Psychic Surgery

"Faith is taking the first step even when you don't see the whole staircase."
— Martin Luther King, Jr.

MOST PEOPLE, UPON FINDING out they have a somewhat serious medical condition, usually make appointments with a specialist and determine their options. I have never been to a doctor about my back. I have, however, been to psychic surgeons in Brazil (and one in Georgia for good measure), Maori healers in New Zealand, an electricity-generating monk in New York City (a good friend of mine, who I hope will forgive the cheeky introduction!), a Sicilian Taoist healer in West Virginia, a Chinese Tui Na practitioner in the Florida Keys, an essential oils clinic in Utah, and a host of chiropractors, acupuncturists, massage therapists, energy workers, and Ro-Hun therapists.

When I was 16, we went to Brazil to meet Mr. Gedes. Beer distributer by day, and trance-channeling, psychic surgeon by night, Mr. Gedes was a tall, smiling man with kind eyes and a comforting manner. I am proof of the last comment, as he spoke no English whatsoever, but somehow persuaded me that instruments the width and length of giant knitting needles could, and should, be inserted into my back without anesthesia. The work Gedes does is surprisingly popular in Brazil. Psychic surgery is considered a spiritual—and specifically Catholic—procedure. Prayer is an important part of the experience, and the people attending sessions are clearly devout believers in God and in the work. Despite its popularity among the people, however, there are stories of intense repression against these miracle workers. And campaigns do exist to discredit the healings they are achieving. As usual, the people must decide for themselves what they are willing to have faith in and what they will walk away from.

Mr. Gedes' office was located in Sao Paolo, the endless city. From our hotel room window, I could not see the edges where the city gave way to farmlands. There was nothing but smog and buildings all the way to the horizon, and when the windows were open the clamoring cacophony of crowded streets was a raucous and blaring reminder of that fact. The sidewalks were dirty and bustling. The streets were overflowing. The cars fought for sovereignty over each other and over the people. The traffic lunged forward and drew up in convulsive bursts and a surge of sooty smoke rose constantly from it.

It is definitely not America.

Sao Paolo has its own rhythm. Not the predictable stop-start, one-two of an American city. Here you must be easy in the knees, swaying and ready. Here the city yields to the chaotic beats, the tempestuous rise and fall of a fretful drummer. Get the thread that binds it all together and hold on tight.

At the edge of the city, in stark contrast to the noisy mayhem, are the endless hills of shantytowns. These are gloomy and still. The plywood, cardboard, and corrugated metal go on for miles. The faces of the people are meek in one moment and defiant in the next and the faces of the shacks are gaping holes onto desolate rooms. A single light bulb hangs from the ceiling in homes lucky enough to have electricity.

Mr. Gedes' office occupied a modest compound just beyond the boundary of the last favela. It was a quaint, nondescript, residential neighborhood. The houses pressed themselves into the street, leaving only a narrow sidewalk, so that you had to move into single file to make way for passersby. You entered the property through an iron gate onto a small, unadorned patio with whitewashed walls and tile floors. Inside is a waiting room, and a smiling woman sits at the desk ready to register your name and your reason for visiting. Once you have accomplished this, you are sent to the treatment room at the back of the house.

It's a communal room, which means that as you are preparing for your own surgery, you have the pleasure of watching Mr. Gedes calmly hammer the knitting needle's monstrous cousin into the yielding anatomies of his courageous patients. Have I mentioned my fear of needles? Considering the procedure, these people were impossibly calm. As I sat among the rows of seekers, I thought to myself that Brazilians must be a profoundly devout and faithful people because even though these surgeries were done in the name of God, I was not basking in the warming mantle of divine love, but chilled by the flashing metal of the giant needles.

"You can go first, mom." I bravely uttered as Gedes tapped another offending needle into a woman's accommodating skull. She didn't even blink.

My mother rolled her eyes. "You are such a drama queen! She's not even reacting! You won't feel a thing."

I couldn't watch the surgeries anymore, so I took a look at the people surrounding us. If they were as unruffled as my mother seemed to be, maybe I could relax a little too. The Brazilians *are* devout. They watched Gedes with genuine longing. They prayed quietly or sat in silent meditation. They were all like me, longing for help, and praying for a miracle. It created a sense of solidarity among us. And as I relaxed into this sense of unity and purpose, the room and the people seemed to develop a holy aspect. A sanctuary was forming for me, and an aura of godliness emanated from this unlikely space. Apart from a cross on the wall and a few lonely pictures of saints, the room was almost entirely fit up with metal, plastic, and vinyl. Rows of chairs fell back from the treatment tables where Gedes worked, and a low wooden wall separated his space from ours; but the churchy feeling was there.

We sat in the nave. He worked in the chancel. We were the congregation, and he was our guide. To the seekers Gedes unveiled the boundary between the limited and the unlimited, the finite and the infinite. He was the crossroads at which all of us will one day find ourselves: the choice to let go for just one moment and have faith that something completely irrational and totally unbelievable is possible. Where is the beauty of life if all our hopes, all our striving, end in death? Somehow, when Mr. Gedes was at work, that linoleum-floored, fluorescent-lit room became a holy retreat, a place where people could come to find the answer.

When it was my turn, I stepped across the threshold and entered Gedes' sanctuary. He gestured for me to approach, and the translator asked for the purpose of my visit. I have always hated that question. I'm embarrassed by my condition. It irritates me when they ask about it. I feel like the victim of extreme impropriety because I don't want to say "scoliosis." I want to say, "Oh, I'm fine, just a check-up, please."

But that has never been the answer. So, I said "scoliosis," and Gedes turned me around to have a look.

"If I straighten this now," he explained "she will be in extreme pain." He ran his hand up and down my spine, feeling the sides, having me bend forward, sideways, backwards.

"It must be done gradually, not all at once. But it will get better."

They guided me to the table, held up a sheet and had me remove my shirt. I lay face down. Gedes came with the needles. Oh, God! Those giant needles! What was I thinking letting my mom talk me into this? How could I be so stupid!

The first insertion came with intense, sharp pain.

"Okay, if this is painless, I'd hate to feel pain."

"Don't worry, Sara, you're doing good!"

"Arrrgggghhh . . . ." The second insertion.

The pain did not lessen as Gedes continued his work, but it released something in me. I was afraid, but I couldn't get up. I thought something could go horribly wrong, but I lay there anyway. I clutched the table and stared at the squares of speckled linoleum. A woman stood by my head with her hands on my shoulders. I stared at her feet. She had nurse shoes on. It comforted me. The theme from *Somewhere in Time* filled the room. That strange and soothing melody inspired my fervid prayers. They say when the heart is full, the tongue cannot contain the flood. I knew my heart was wretched with longing. I longed for healing. I longed for freedom, for a fearless life where hope did not feel like a treacherous emotion. I tried to forget the pain and focused on begging the spirits working with Gedes to help me.

As Gedes worked, the sting of the needles was reduced to a slight discomfort. He said the pain was due to the stuck energy in my spine. Energetically speaking, my back had gone years without any movement. I was raised on talk like this. It was not a strange thing to hear, and I knew perfectly what he meant. Of course creating movement now would hurt. Think of how you feel the day after a yoga class. Sore, right? Take that soreness, multiply by a hundred, squeeze it into an angry little ball and then shove it into your back with a needle. Now you know.

They gave me my shirt, and I sat on the table for a moment. Gedes again looked at my back. He told the translator, and she told me, that when I started having kids, I would see a big change.

"Won't she have problems with carrying a baby?"

"No, not at all. It will help the spine, like 24-hour traction." Gedes smiled and patted my shoulder. "She should have lots of babies. Well, no more than four, though."

"Why only four?" The lady in nurse shoes looked concerned. Gedes laughed.

"I'm teasing! She can have four, five, six . . . however many she wants. Her spine is going to get better."

We thanked Mr. Gedes for his help and headed back to Sao Paolo.

My mother was in high spirits.

"Well, I don't need to know anything else. Mr. Gedes says it will get better, and I believe him."

Through the years, we made several trips to Mr. Gedes' healing sanctuary before he passed away in 2003. With his help, I found the courage to hope. I found the strength to forge my way where there is no path, where there is no guarantee. Just faith.

You may have noticed that if you venture beyond the dominant belief system, especially when it comes to healing, the alternative path can seem endlessly winding and cluttered. Everyone has a brilliant insight—a tidbit they got in meditation or a wise word from an "amazing" teacher. There is a vast amount of information out there and seemingly no way of knowing what is valuable and what is misguided silliness.

Intelligently navigating the new-age milieu has become a lifelong quest, and discernment is a must because my health is always at stake. But I have found that one thing is paramount in the pursuit of truth, and that is experience. There is no shift that happens without experience. Grasping something intellectually may feel rewarding, but it has never shaken the core of my being like an *experience* of truth. People often use the intellect to distinguish a falsehood or a fraud from a truth, but this is an unfortunate mistake. The intellect is governed by the ego, and the ego is bound by fear. We don't usually uncover a truth about ourselves in the absence of fear or insecurity. In fact, many times, when you encounter an individual who has experienced a true transformation of self or a true healing, they usually have stories of overcoming fear. They often talk about the ridicule they endured and the loneliness they felt as they pursued a certain course of action. But always inside they were propelled forward, against all resistance. Even ignoring their own trepidation, they continued forward. I once asked a friend, who seemed so confident and daring to me, how she was able to go through life with no fear. She told me she had a lot of fear, but she always chose to ignore it. "Otherwise," she said, "I would never do anything with my life."

Everyone experiences fear. It's those who ignore it who have a chance to lead truly remarkable lives. I say embrace the unfamiliar, and see where it leads you. Maybe you'll have a deeply transformative experience. At least you may go on a couple good adventures.

During all of our journeys to Brazil, I had a chance to experience some of the religious culture. Religion in Brazil is a grab bag of astral energies, Godly love, and human artistry. "God in heaven" just doesn't sound right in Brazil. Palpable, bright, alive and all around you: that's God in Brazil. Where else, but in a place like this, can a man go into trance, claim to be embodied by an "entity" and proceed to cut fully conscious people wide open in front of hundreds of devoted Catholics and do all of it in the name of God with no fear for his safety and no objection from the crowd? Can you imagine the storm of righteous fanaticism this would elicit in America? But these things are going on every day, all over Brazil. They love it! Brazilians aren't afraid to embrace life. They see God wherever there is good.

We visited several churches on one of our trips to Brazil. There are so many whimsical and engaging churches there, but most remarkable was the Dom Bosco Church in Brasilia. It is a perfect cube, constructed entirely of slender stone beams surrounded by cobalt blue and purple glass. The effect is astonishing as you enter the nave, as if the building were enveloped by the evening sky. A chandelier, a massive, glowing thing, hangs at the center of this man-made firmament and casts an ethereal light throughout the room as if the stars themselves were lighting it. I walked silently to a pew and could not resist the temptation to kneel on that little ledge, the hallmark of Catholic piety. How to share these strange experiences?

As I knelt there, silent in my thoughts, an energy began to condense just behind me, like a consciousness forming, making itself known to me. I did not turn to see it, but I knew that it was golden and glowing with intensity. If I had turned, I would not have *seen* it anyway, because it was not dense in the physical sense. It was intelligent energy, alive and powerful. So powerful, in fact, that as it approached I feared for my small human life. This force, this potent intelligence, seemed perfectly capable of lovingly tearing my soul—or more probably my ego—into tiny little shreds, but it stayed back, maybe ten feet. It hovered behind me. That pure, uninhibited, *intelligent* light was the most powerful thing I had ever experienced. After we left, I felt a bit guilty that I had not allowed the energy to come closer. Maybe I could have experienced healing. Maybe things would be different if I hadn't been so afraid.

Fear does not keep you safe. It only holds you back. When you begin to open up and allow for something unfamiliar in your life, something you may fear, you have a better chance of experiencing truth. I mention this because I spend so much time worrying, so much time in uncertainty, that I prize the moments when I can say "this is it, this one piece of the puzzle is solved." I feel released from fear when I come to a realization about my own harmful belief systems or when I find a healer who is implementing real change in my body. At those times, I see the value of the path I have chosen. I understand how much I'm learning. These little breakthroughs come in all shapes and sizes. I am always grappling with the natural laws—the law of attraction, divine providence, anatomy, and physiology. Nothing is too far out. Nothing is unrelated to the all-consuming quest to understand my life. And the more earnest I am in my quest, the more open I become to every possibility. The more open I am, the more every moment appears as an opportunity to experience grace. But these moments of grace don't occur unless I break free from my habitual perspective: my "comfort zone." You have to open up in order to see some change.

Not too long ago, I visited Santiago de Compostela, a sacred pilgrimage site on the northwestern coast of Spain. Brecht and I were staying with friends in a city about a four-hour drive away, and we left for Santiago before dawn in hopes of having as much time there as possible. That morning, armed with steaming coffee and fresh bread, Brecht artfully steered the car through the lush green, hills of northern Spain, and I focused on what I wanted to achieve that day. I don't know if it was the peaceful setting or the fact that we were headed for one of the most famous pilgrim-age destinations in Europe, but I found myself praying ardently. Brecht began to tell me about the tradition of pilgrimages to Santiago de Compostela. It is one of the most western points of Europe, and people have always walked there. The tradition is that when you arrive you give your troubles to the setting sun in the west and return home (towards the east) to begin a new life. I thought about that for a moment and suddenly with tears in my eyes said, "I wish I could leave my troubles behind me."

With this wish in mind, I kept saying to myself, "Please, help me to unload my burdens. Help me to be free." Over and over I thought it, in sincerity and with no expectation. Just good, honest prayer, though I have never considered myself to be religious. We arrived at the cathedral, and inside they were having a mass. It was in Spanish and, as I am unfamiliar with the Catholic protocol and I couldn't understand much of the language, I simply sat with Brecht in an out of the way pew and observed the proceedings.

The cathedral is huge. There are various chapels along the periphery, each one devoted to a saint or the Virgin Mary or an angel; each one with beautiful stone arches, paintings, and sculptures in wood or in gold. It's truly an amazing place, if you like churches, and I love going into old churches. There is something about a place that for hundreds of years has inspired awe and humility in the people entering it. The love in the hearts of those people has energized the place. I often wonder: do the old cathedrals carry so much energy simply because the people have worshiped there for so many centuries; or is there an intelligent energy there in response to the constant prayers which have flowed from the hearts of thousands as they entered this sacred ground? Are we all alone here with no one to guide us but each other or is there a higher intelligence that we can depend on as we go through life? When I am in a place like the cathedral at Santiago, I find myself truly adoring God and the wellspring of love that gives life to everything.

In the back of the cathedral, behind the altar, you can enter through a small doorway a stairwell leading up to the statue of St. James, overlaid with precious metals and stones. People line up in this little corridor to touch the statue and ask for help, healing, or simply to give thanks for blessings. All day, people can be seen entering and exiting this tiny room. I also wanted a chance to experience this little ritual. I had done it a few years before, but not much had happened that time. This morning, however, I had been praying so eagerly I thought perhaps the experience would be different. Of course, as we entered there was a line in front of us. Brecht was busy snapping pictures of everything in the cramped corridor and I was slowly climbing the stairway, waiting for my moment with the holy statue. As we entered the little room, I touched the back of St. James (he faces outward over the cathedral, and you pass behind him) and looked at Brecht, who was holding the camera up for more pictures. Suddenly, I could feel emotion welling up in me. Such a feeling of strength and compassion filled the room that I couldn't keep myself from crying. I was overwhelmed with gratitude. It was not just a feeling of union with this infinite love that brought me to blissful tears, but a feeling of RE-union. Somehow, I recognized this loving energy, and I knew it would hold me and take care of me forever.

As I stood there with my hand on the statue and tears rolling down my cheeks, Brecht came and put his arm around me and placed his hand on the statue too. I let the feelings of love and peace that had suddenly filled the little room wash over me, taking away my fears and worries. Thankfully, perhaps blessedly, no one entered the space as we stood there in each other's arms. I could see them at the bottom of the stairs passing by and peering in, but no one chose to enter. A space that is usually filled with people remained empty for those moments. To me it was a sacred experience, a small miracle. In this private moment, I forgave myself for all of my mistakes, for all of my worrying, and for the first time I allowed the strength of God to carry me. It felt amazing to rely on something so strong and so beautiful to guide me.

Until that moment, I was unaware that I was suffering so much. With this sudden unburdening, I could now acknowledge that I had felt profoundly alone. To me, the world was callous and unfeeling, and I was helpless to change it. I was terrified of letting go because control over my environment was the only thing that made me feel safe. A lamb might be led to the slaughter, but I wasn't about to be. I held onto everything as tightly as I could. I eliminated variables as much as I could, and I tried to feel comfortable within these boundaries.

What's so amazing is that I had no idea I was doing that. How could I know? We all bury our fears, and it's easy to understand why. We couldn't live day to day with full awareness of such a heavy burden. The pain would be far too great to bear. In my ignorance, I was terrified of losing control. I believed the opposite of having control was annihilation, not freedom. I'm talking about the fear of death, a fear that permeates the core of the collective psyche. Who could have the courage to even look at such a fear, much less change it? We all have fears like these. Fears we don't know about. Fears we put in place to ensure our survival. We never question the resulting behavior, because we're unaware of the source of these compulsions. The behavior becomes entrenched, and we assume it is natural because we are unconscious of the source.

The only thing that could shake me into consciousness was an experience that made me feel so safe and so loved, that I had the courage to acknowledge these fears. Standing in the cathedral that day, I realized that something was awry. Enmeshed in my fear, I wasn't capable of grasping the truth. Thankfully, I experienced a powerful and loving presence at Santiago, and it gave me a new perspective. The truth is we are never "going it alone." There is something to lean on, something to call on, and it infuses everything, gives life to everything. We are a part of this energy we call God or Allah or, simply, "the universe." Whatever you call it, this loving presence creates our lives through us. We are supported. We are loved by life itself, by this grand and bountiful existence. *We belong here* and there is nothing to fear.

Instead of fear, try acceptance. Acceptance is the joyful result of your awareness that God is in all things. I came to this awareness through many experiences; and in these moments, I knew that the world was wholly divine and in perfect order. Think about it: if there is nothing outside of God, including yourself, then there is nothing for you to improve. You can allow everything to be as it is. As soon as you give up your throne, you can participate in the infinite joy, love, and perfection that exist in the world. Is there something more sacred and perfect than life itself? Is there something more beautiful than the trees or the sky or you? How easily we forget the sheer magnitude of life. How hard it is for us to see the good when we focus so intently on the bad. Life is grand, and it is ours to enjoy. So, acceptance of life isn't a task or a sacrifice. It is a gift.

Consider what would happen if you really acknowledged that something more intelligent than you created this world: you would begin to interact with it in a very different way. How your perspective would change if you knew that the people in your life and everything that is happening to you, everything that you observe around you, is a manifestation of the divine order of this universe. Wouldn't the quality of your interactions change drastically? The world looks a lot different to someone who is humble and loving than it does to someone who feels disempowered and angry.

Last year I volunteered at a meditation program Brecht was attending. It was just two days and one night, but I felt like I was there for an eternity. I was pretty okay for the first part of the day. Brecht was in class, and I was working in the kitchen. I like working in a kitchen. I feel comfortable. I know what I'm supposed to do. I worked in the kitchen of my parents' restaurant when I was in high school, so the large, industrial kitchen at the ashram did not intimidate me. I just went straight to work. However, after my shift at the kitchen, I suddenly grew so tired and at the same time anxious. I missed Brecht. That was certain, but there was something else bothering me. As I walked back from the kitchen to the dorms, I tried to pay attention to my emotions. I was definitely bothered, but I wasn't angry. It was more like intense anxiety, and I was feeling bad about myself because of it. I thought about al of the people who could just enjoy the ashram experience with no trouble. They would love the novelty of it. They would relish the change from their daily lives, and they would feel grateful for the spiritual experiences they were having. Like kids at a summer camp, nothing would bother them; but I was feeling challenged by everything. I was sick of being uncomfortable, for one.

It was freezing outside, and the ashram, located on a plateau in the mountains, was besieged by an unceasing wind. We, the volunteers, had our meals in a partially constructed building with walls of plastic, and the wind beat mercilessly against them. At dinner, we huddled around a propane heater seated in folding chairs with our plates balanced on our laps. Normally, I would have made a silly remark about how ridiculous the whole thing was, but no one said a word. Although I was surrounded by people, I experienced the meal as though in solitude.

I couldn't see Brecht at all, and, worst of all, I couldn't sleep next to him. We hadn't spent more than a few hours apart in a year. I hated the idea of spending my first night without him in an atmosphere that was so challenging for me. My back was acting up too, and I was in incredible pain. I didn't know what to blame that on. I had worked in the kitchen for about four hours, but I often spent long periods of time in my own kitchen, and I never experienced anything like this. I lay in bed trying all of the positions that usually relieve tension in my back. Nothing worked. My head was aching, and at the same time, my heart was racing. I could feel my pulse pounding in my ears, and a sickening feeling was rising up in me. It wasn't nausea. It was more like dread. I thought if I could cry that might relieve some tension, but no tears came. I just kept turning round and round.

What could make me feel this way? Was I so attached to Brecht that one night away from him was enough to create so much turmoil? Was there something about the ashram that still triggered me? Whatever it was something was pushing me to what I felt like was the brink of insanity.

I sat up and put my feet on the floor. The tiles were cold, but the feeling grounded me. I took a few deep breaths and ran my fingers through my hair. Brecht was in the next building probably sleeping like a baby. He's always easy. His favorite thing to say is, "I'm easy." When I felt a little steadier, I walked to the bathroom to look at myself in the mirror. My face showed no sign of the emotional struggle inside. I lifted my shirt and turned to look at my back. It was a little red, which was strange, and the muscles were taut. I turned around and stared at my face again. My shoulders were even. My ears were even. These were the things I had started to use as benchmarks of alignment, and everything looked pretty good. I splashed some water on my face, and then I kept staring. I wanted to glean some understanding from my reflection, but it was clear that whatever was bothering me would remain a mystery for now. I switched off the bathroom light and walked back to my bed.

The next morning I was awakened at five, as everybody got ready for morning prayers. We all dressed warmly and silently trod to the meditation hall. I sat towards the back so that when Brecht walked in he would see me. For me, it was like a reunion after months of separation. I couldn't believe I was feeling so dependent. I had always believed I was the one keeping everything together. Now, I was very much awakened to the fact that Brecht was also contributing a significant measure of sanity to our marriage.

We sat on the floor together and listened to the residents chanting. The meditation hall is a 39,000-square-foot dome, and the acoustics are incredible. Their voices echoed around us with an eerie majesty. I didn't know the chant, but my mood lifted with the beauty of the singing. I felt peaceful in that moment and happily joined in as everyone bent forward to place their foreheads on the ground in reverence. Suddenly, my back released and all the vertebrae that had been bothering me let out a series of cracks and pops. The struggle was finally over.

Later that day, I was visiting Brecht near the men's dorm. I told him about my experiences the night before and about the release I had that morning. He said I probably had trouble with the fact that everything at the ashram was rooted in submission and acceptance. That sounded very reasonable to me, and it reminded me of my first time at this particular ashram. I was there for a meditation program, and upon arrival I had to give up my cell phone and car keys for the weekend. I had a very hard time accepting this. I thought maybe I had mistakenly joined a cult, and I spent the entire time at this retreat in a mild rage. I believed in the guru's teachings, but I had no faith at all in his methods.

The thing that really broke me happened on the last day. I had to pee, and no one would let me go. I thought, well, they'll give a break. An hour went by, no break. Two hours, same thing. Finally, four hours had gone by and still no break. I was angry, I was in intense pain and I felt completely trapped. It seemed like there was nothing I could do. They would just force me to sit there until my bladder burst, and this was supposed to be part of my spiritual growth? After a week of being furious and frustrated, this was the last straw for me. I just couldn't take anymore. Then, suddenly, something in me snapped. Somehow, I gave up control. It was clear I wasn't going to get my way. There was nothing for me to do. So, I decided to do nothing. I totally let go of the need to control my environment and it felt amazing. Throughout the week Sadhguru had mentioned his wish that we all make just a small crack in our egos. He hoped we could all experience the weightlessness that comes from giving up just a small bit of our precious autonomy. He said the program was designed to impose upon these boundaries, so that we could learn the full extent of our limitations.

It's counterintuitive, but when I allowed this imposition, I felt such joy and freedom that it brought tears to my eyes. I didn't stop crying for seven hours. Have you ever cried for seven hours? You get a splitting headache at the end of it. But I was so happy I didn't care. On the plane ride home I didn't read or listen to music or strike up a conversation. I just sat there in utter bliss, feeling totally connected to every passenger. Even the plane itself seemed special and deserving of love. For weeks the idea of "entertainment" seemed totally redundant. Life itself, just being alive, was more entertainment than I could ever want. My mom was worried that I might disappear into the mountains and never come back. All of this, just from taking a small leap of faith and giving up a little control!

Soon after attending this program, and while I was still in the midst of that blissful state, I went to visit my chiropractor. When I arrived in the treatment room, she had my X-ray hanging on the wall. Usually, the sight of it makes me cringe, and I spend the majority of the appointment avoiding looking at it; but this time as I stared at my curvy spine, I felt a genuinely loving connection to it. Debbie had left the room for a moment, and this gave me a chance to really stare at the X-ray. As I allowed my eyes to drift along the biggest curve, I realized that I almost never felt loving towards my spine. Let me rephrase that: not "almost never," I realized I NEVER felt loving towards my spine. The only emotion I had for my spine was anger and hatred. As I allowed this new feeling of love to wash over me, I got tears in my eyes thinking of all the time I had wasted hating this part of me. How could I heal, I wondered, if I was filled with hatred and resentment? Could I let these feelings go and, instead, cultivate the love I was experiencing now? This was *my* spine. It was a part of me. Suddenly hating my spine felt akin to hating a little child. I wanted more than anything to transcend that hatred and develop a trusting and loving relationship with my body. In that instant, my spine abruptly shifted from a dreaded enemy to a long-lost friend. It was a powerful reconnection to a part of myself that I had been abusing for years.

6

Hohepa/Maori Healing

"All human wisdom is contained in these two words, 'Wait and Hope'."
—Alexandre Dumas

SIX YEARS AFTER VISITING Gedes, I was 22 and living in Boston. I was on the brink of pursuing a master's degree in Acupuncture and Oriental Medicine and struggling through a pre-med program at Tufts University. I did yoga and Qi Gong, meditated daily, went to a so-so chiropractor and worked at an independent coffee shop with a devout following and an impending bankruptcy issue. It's now a crepe shop, as far as I know. One day, my mother received a phone call from a friend in California who had met a group of Maori healers. They were coming to stay at her sister's house for a week, and my mother was invited to experience their healings and ceremonies. She flew to L.A. a couple months later and immediately fell in love with the people and their incredible healing abilities. Seeing the profound work that was being accomplished, she mentioned my back problems, and one of the women in the group said she should bring me to New Zealand to meet Papa, their teacher. Naturally, when she returned home she called me immediately and said we had to go to New Zealand as soon as possible. I acquiesced—who wouldn't? And within a few weeks, we were bound out of L.A. on New Zealand Air for Auckland, New Zealand.

The plane ride was long—thirteen hours—but I had never been in such a beautiful cabin before. My mother had so many frequent flier miles that she managed to upgrade us to first class. I think the cabin was bigger than my apartment at the time. It was huge! My chair extended into a fully flat position and did not come near the seat in front of me. I was grateful beyond belief for this because I could not imagine thirteen hours crammed into a little seat in coach—not with my back. It would have been terrible. The cabin was not only amazing, but the food was delicious. In particular, I remember being pleasantly surprised when the flight attendant wheeled her cart up to us and offered me organic strawberry yogurt. Now I see organic products on Delta from time to time, but ten years ago I had never seen anything like this. Delicious, organic food on an airplane? If the national airline was any reflection on the country, I thought I could be very happy there.

At the thirteenth hour, the plane descended through the final layer of clouds, and I marveled at the lush green land and the gorgeous bright blue hues of the ocean below us. I had never seen any pictures of New Zealand, and I hadn't known what to expect. This was like a tropical paradise. I couldn't take my eyes off of it. I furiously snapped pictures from the plane window, wanting to capture the freshness, the beauty of this marvelous land. I was eager to get on the ground and explore, but I also hated the idea of giving up this amazing vista. It was magical.

We landed smoothly, slogged our way through customs and baggage claim, met our hosts, Ata and Paraone, and immediately got on our way to meet Papa. Hohepa de la Mer, or Papa as he was known affectionately, had sparkling mischievous eyes and a beaming smile. Joy and contentment emanated from him in a way that I had never seen from anyone else. He was pure, unadulterated joy, and I loved him immediately. He was also huge. Maori people seem to be big as a rule, but Papa was even big for a Maori. He was tall, hefty, and imposing. His hair was wild and curly and I never saw him wear anything other than a sweat suit. If you saw him on the street, you probably wouldn't think he was a world-class healer with incredible spiritual abilities. But what does someone like that look like anyway?

I was surprised at how quickly I felt connected to Papa. When I met him I felt as though I was reestablishing a relationship with a long-lost friend. I don't know how he felt about me, but I always felt that he treated me like a daughter. I often wondered, what could a Maori healer in his sixties and an American girl in her early twenties possibly have in common? How could I feel so comfortable and so close to someone who was so vastly different from me?

Years later, after Papa passed away, I was at Delphi attending a trance channeling session with Marshall Smith, the husband of the founder of Delphi. He channeled Arthur Ford, a close friend of the founder's who had died in 1971. This particular session was special because Arthur allowed us to call on family and friends who had passed on. We gave him a name and our relationship to the person and he would do his best to bring them through. When it was my turn to go, I had so many people that I wanted to call on, but for some reason I decided to call on

Papa. I took my place in the middle of the circle of people and told Arthur, "I'd like to call on Hohepa De La Mer."

To which Arthur replied, "On *who?* Hopa?"

"No, Arthur, Ho-*Hepa.*"

"Is that a name?"

The crowd was starting to giggle at this point.

"Arthur," I giggled along, "It's a Maori healer from New Zealand. You can try calling him Papa, that's what we all called him, anyway."

"Oh, is this your father?"

"No, Arthur."

"Okay, okay, let me see what I can do . . . ."

There was silence for a while and I didn't know if he would find him or not. But eventually he returned with a man who he described as "huge with crazy hair and no shoes on." I had to laugh, Maoris often go without shoes, even in the middle of the city.

"Is this who you are looking for?" Arthur seemed doubtful.

"Yes it is, Arthur! Thank you!"

He then told me that Papa wanted me to know that he only came through because it was me asking for him. He said there were many people waiting for me to begin my healing work, and that my hands were filled with healing energy, and I needed to share this with the world.

It was a short message, but what struck me was that he said he only came through because it was me calling. I thought back to the times I had spent with Papa, and realized that our connection was real, however unlikely it seemed.

My first session with Papa took place in his office in Aukland. It was a small room, and Papa, several of his students, my mother and I all squeezed in together for the event. They asked me to lay face down on the table with my shirt off. Just as I was placing my head in the face cradle, I noticed Papa gathering some tools: a few fist-sized rocks and a very large club-like piece of wood that had been hanging on the wall. As he removed the club, he casually mentioned that a Hawaiian chief had given it to him years ago, and this would be his first time needing to use it. Although it looked like a very mean piece of wood, I trusted Papa implicitly and remained as I was.

He began slowly: kneading my muscles, lifting my legs, working up my spine. Then he took a rock from the pile and began rubbing it firmly along the taut muscles of my lower back. This might sound pleasant to someone who has had a hot stone massage, but don't get the wrong idea. A hot stone massage is so relaxing. They lather you up with oil and the rocks are pleasantly warm and smooth. It feels wonderful. This was excruciating. As he worked he told me that he did not want to use any oil because he needed the friction of the rock against my skin to break through the calcification. Ata was sitting at the head of the table and her knees were just under my face. When I opened my eyes, I saw that her pants were drenched by the drool that was endlessly flowing from me. It sounds gross, I know, but I wasn't aware of anything except the burning pain in my back. Suddenly, he stopped working and grasped something in my muscle tissue. "There," he said "this is her kidney. It has been trapped in this calcification for years, and we needed to free it before we could do anything else."

A few days later, we planned a weekend trip to the Marae for a healing class with Papa. A Marae is a communal space within a Maori community. Important social events occur there, ceremonies are performed there, inter-tribal meetings may be held there, and like in our case, healing work can be conducted there. We made the three-hour trip to the Marae by car. One of Papa's students, Eddie, was at the wheel, and Papa sat in the passenger seat. I love a long car ride, and I relished the chance to take in more of the magical New Zealand landscape. However, most of the trip, my mom and I gripped the door handles of the back seat as Eddie flew down the road at impossible speeds. Papa and Eddie chatted casually, and my mom and I exchanged harrowed looks.

I was happy being in such close quarters with Papa, who was always a joy to be around. It made me happy just to listen to his stories and hear his opinion on just about anything. There is something so special about people like Papa who are so light and easy that just being near them is inspirational. They have very few hang-ups and lack the emotional baggage that we all seem to carry around with us endlessly. When I was around Papa, I felt safe enough to let go of everything that ever bothered me and just be in the moment. The memory of that feeling has never left me. I would have moved to New Zealand in a heartbeat if they had suggested it to me.

When we arrived at the Marae, Papa explained the significance of the architecture. The arms extending from the tip of the roof represent the Marae's purpose of embracing and safeguarding the community. Everything about the Marae had a meaning. The carvings, the spaces within and outside of it . . . there was nothing about the building and its surroundings that was not imbued with purpose and intention.

We began class immediately. There were students as well as members of the community who had come to receive healings from the class. I was one of those to be worked on, and when they called me forward, I lay on the massage table at the front of the room. As I lay there, Papa explained some things about scoliosis and the healing work in general. Then he lifted my shirt to reveal my back and said "what would you do to straighten this?" The students oohed and ahhed for a moment and then he had them all take a turn placing their hands on me and discovering what they could about my condition. Normally, I would not have been able to endure this kind of display, but I had such tremendous respect for Papa and I could feel the loving respect each of these students had for their very vulnerable patient that I was able to relax and enjoy all of the attention.

Each student had a different reaction to what they were feeling. Some were more clinical than others, telling Papa about the movement of energy or the flexibility of my muscles. Others were far more emotional, and one woman burst into tears as she placed her hands on me. Through her sobs she told Papa she felt the conflict between her people (indigenous tribes) and my people (white people). He seemed to understand her completely, but I wondered what that could possibly have to do with my spine. Why would she feel that in me? I had no direct experiences of that conflict. I had no indigenous blood. The only connection I had was a great grandmother who had been very close to the Seneca tribe when she was alive, but even though my mother was very close with her, I never met her. She passed away long before I was born.

The students continued to take turns working on me, and then it was time for lunch. After a lunch of smoked fish, vegetables, and a stew made of various meats and one unidentified animal's spinal column—being largely vegetarian, I did not venture to taste that—we headed back to the healing tables. Once again I lay face down and the students began working on me. Papa sat at the head of the room overseeing everything. As I lay there, I became aware of a very strong presence standing just at the head of my table. I thought maybe Papa had come over but when I opened my eyes to peek, there was no one standing there. I have always been good at sensing spirit, and I figured someone was paying me a visit. I had the distinct impression that he was of Native American descent. This did not completely surprise me, given the student's reaction earlier. And I did have a few occasions in my life when, looking in the rear view mirror of my car, I had to control my shock and avoid swerving from the road because an Indian had unexpectedly appeared in the back seat.

I enjoyed his presence, but I didn't say anything about it. I figured it was for me to experience and nothing else. But these Maori healers . . . whereas I only sensed his presence, they actually saw something remarkable. I don't know if it's the way they are raised or something in the gene pool, but so many of them are incredibly clairvoyant. I had not been aware of this man standing in front of me for more than a minute, when Papa said to everyone, "We have some visitors." They all looked towards the head of the room, where I am told an entire tribe of Native Americans had entered. They stood in full regalia at the head of my table and announced that I was their daughter and they came to see the work that was being done and to honor the Maori.

The Marae is a sacred space, a place for such inter-tribal meetings to take place. This was not only an appearance for my sake, but something incredibly special for everyone who was there that day. I only wished that I could have seen them the way the others had.

That evening we slept in the Marae. The women gathered together on one side and the men on the other. We all had our own sleeping mats and blankets, which we lined up next to each other on the floor. I loved the communal feeling, and I was tickled to be sleeping in such a sacred space with such wonderful people all around me.

The next morning a woman came with her twin boys, who were just learning to crawl. One of the boys did this perfectly. He moved all over the place charming everyone. The other was unable to crawl because his leg was set at a strange angle. He had to swing this leg around in a strange circular pattern in order to move anywhere. He was understandably frustrated and cried non-stop. Papa took him to one of the healing tables and began working with him gently. It didn't take long before the baby was cooing happily and enjoying Papa's loving presence. Papa worked on his pelvis for a while until the baby fell into a restful sleep, and when he woke up, he could crawl! His little face was beaming. I thought if Papa hadn't been here, maybe this child would have grown up with a terrible deformity. Yet it was so easily fixed! How many other problems like this could be fixed in infancy with no trouble at all. I have often wished that I had been near Papa as a baby. I too might have been healed in one short session.

On the last day of our trip, we all gathered into several cars to make our way to a hill where Papa would conduct a ceremony. I wasn't sure what the purpose was or how I would feel afterwards. I only knew that it was one of many sacred ceremonies conducted by the Maori Shaman throughout the year. I think it was a cleansing for the community.

I rode up with Eddie, sitting in the back seat of his car with my mother. As we drove along, I enjoyed the vibrant greens of the surrounding landscape. New Zealand is so beautiful and so different from America. In fact, it's incomparable to any place I've been. When you go to Europe, the landscape is not all that different. Maybe they have more of one variety of tree and less of another, but New Zealand is like another planet. The trees and plants are totally different, and to me everything seemed so alive and exquisitely colorful.

When we got to the base of the hill everyone gathered around Papa and waited for his instructions. He told us to climb to the top, remove our shoes, and stand in two circles with the women in the middle facing towards the center and the men on the outside, their backs to the women. We did as were told and followed a path the rest of the way up the hill. From the top you could see the surrounding country for miles. The day was bright and sunny. Everything was richly green and intensely alive. Even I could see that this was a quiet, but powerful place. When we had formed our circles, Papa told us to join hands and close our eyes.

Then the sounds began. They started as a soft hum; barely a word was formed. It was just the soft melodious vibration of a Shaman's communication with nature; a primordial resonance that emanated from Papa and travelled deep into the earth. As his humming grew louder, the others began to join in. I tried to empty my head of thoughts and focus instead on the undulating pattern created by the voices surrounding me. The women started to chant slowly and steadily in Maori, leaving no silent spaces during the chanting, as if each person was responsible for filling in the silence with a voice. I listened and wished that I knew the chant.

The men joined after the women had completed one cycle of song. It was a richer sound than the women produced, but the two pitches together were nicely balanced. I could hear Papa's voice above the others. It was strong and sure, and I felt supported by it and by the community and the hand-holding and the weaving together of everyone's voices.

Suddenly, the light grew darker and I stealthily opened my eyes to see what had happened. As I did, I felt the first raindrop land on my shoulder, and then we were all drenched. The rain was falling in thick sheets and I had to close my eyes again. I wondered if the sudden storm was part of the ceremony. Did Papa call the rain? The wind whipped around the top of the hill in a chaotic dance, and I imagined all of our shoes flying away on the strong air currents. I was happy I had worn sandals and didn't have to think about soggy shoes for the trip back.

Everyone continued to chant, and the feeling behind the words was even more intense with the unexpected weather. My mom was standing to my right, and she squeezed my hand as the rain fell harder. I squeezed back and lifted my head so the rain could fall more directly on my face. This whole ceremony was designed to strengthen the community. I wondered if that had an impact on their daily lives. The women standing in the center of the circle clearly played a central role in the sustenance and survival of the whole. The men faced outward, communicating more directly with the outer world and protecting the sacred center. Were relationships structured in this way too? I liked this idea and wished that Americans weren't so narrow-minded and principled.

The rain was still falling heavily when Papa stopped singing and told everyone to gather their troubles, worries, and painful memories from the previous year and let them go. His voice thundered over the down-pour as he said, "Let the rain purify you. Make the decision now to drop these burdens. Let them soak into the earth; the rain will cleanse her of your negative beliefs."

As the ceremony came to an end, the clouds began to separate and the countryside was bright and sunny once more. We followed the path down the hill and back to our cars. I knew these were the last moments I had with Papa, as we were heading to the airport directly from there. I wanted to express all of my gratitude for the amazing work and the wonderful way in which he and his students welcomed us into their community. Instead, I just started crying and gave everyone a big hug. I watched with tears streaming down my face as Papa got into a car. He smiled warmly through the window and waved as they drove away.

That was the last I ever saw of Papa. He passed away a couple years later before we could make it back to New Zealand for another visit.

During that trip, I wasn't aware of any major changes in my back. But on the plane ride home—not first class!—I realized that I was experiencing almost no discomfort. Those were the easiest thirteen hours I had ever been through. I couldn't believe it! This was definitely a first. Of all the healings I had ever had, Papa's work had created the biggest shift in my daily experience. For the first time, I felt truly hopeful, and that was a wonderful blessing.

A couple weeks later I was going out to dinner with my family. I had a dress on and heels, and I was looking in the mirror one last time when I noticed a striking difference in the appearance of my legs. I didn't realize before that the muscles in my calves were undefined, but now I could see clearly that my ankles were thinner and my muscles were well formed and elegant. I took the heels off to make sure it wasn't a trick of the eye. Nope! My legs had literally transformed overnight. Was this also the result of Papa's work? I was still enjoying a level of comfort that I had never experienced before, and this seemed to be another physical sign that my body was capable of recovery. I had never had this kind of hard evidence before. I felt buoyed by the changes, and hungry for more.

7

Cheryl

"Surrender simply means trust, relaxing.
It is an attitude rather than an act: you live through trust."
—Osho

THERE IS A SPIRITUALIST church in Wheeling, West Virginia, a large, beige brick building that has survived a century of rezoning, demolishing, and flooding. It is old, but the loving care of its parishioners has helped it maintain its dignity while the houses that were once its stately neighbors have sunken, feebly, into disrepair. Adjacent to the church is a small, unassuming parsonage. It is a white, one-story ensemble with a small yard enclosed by a chain-link fence. A cement walk leads from the fence to a raised porch where you find the front door. It is here in this parsonage that I first met the petite, spunky Sicilian woman with the untamable jet-black hair and the attitude to match.

Every day, usually before I've managed a cup of coffee, Cheryl appears in lavish eye makeup and bright red lipstick (she never travels without her giant, light-up makeup mirror). She is always dressed in black from head to toe, sparkling with earrings, rings and bracelets. She is never without her platform shoes. She tucks her eye drops into her bra. She wears shoulder pads with everything. Her cappuccino maker is a constant companion, and she has promised me, several times, that she will one day make me some really excellent pasta fazool.

On our first meeting, Brecht and I stepped through the doorway of the parsonage into a tiny hallway. Immediately, we came upon an altar with incense and votive candles. To the left were a bathroom and three bedrooms and to the right was a small living room filled to bursting with a giant, black leather sectional, two old-fashioned armchairs, and a massive TV. Several lamps were placed around the room along with a sideboard filled with knick-knacks and artwork on the walls. I sought a position on the sofa and tentatively peeked into the kitchen, which was also filled with furniture. Cheryl immediately began talking about how she met my mom and how she didn't know whether she should take me on or not; but something in her said she had to.

"Honey, I just knew you were going to be something special in my life. I really did! Here fill this out."

She handed both of us some health history forms.

"You know, I told your mom, if Sara's not serious then I don't want to work with her, but she said you were very serious; and when she said that I believed her, okay, honey? Something in me just knew."

I agreed. "I am serious, very serious. I want to be rid of this." She turned to Brecht.

"So you want treatments, too? This is perfect. I've been waiting for people like you! It's wonderful to go through healing together. You know what I mean: everything just comes together then."

As we talked about my goals for my back, I started to get the feeling that working with Cheryl wasn't just about the treatments. Her goal was life-transformation: to gather my life into her adept hands and sculpt from the fear and hopelessness something fine and bright. I think you could call it wisdom, and when I am with Cheryl I feel encouraged to make this shift.

"Alchemy," said Cheryl. "We're doing alchemy."

After a short discussion, Cheryl led us down the small hallway to the treatment room. I said it was fine for Brecht to join us. We entered a small, white room with a treatment table in the center. The décor suggested an Asian influence, but it wasn't overdone. No red lanterns hung from the ceiling. Brecht sat on a stool in the corner and I took the very familiar position lying on the treatment table.

By now I'm an expert when it comes to determining the skill level of any body worker. I've seen so many! Cheryl was good. That was obvious. As she worked, I felt totally at ease, even as she twisted and stretched my limbs into knots. But I was really impressed when a thick greasy fluid started coming out of me, right near the curvature in my spine, where her hands were. It's difficult to explain such a thing, but it was like ectoplasm would be: not quite physical but definitely there and real. It felt wet. I felt like my body was wet, and Cheryl's hands seemed wet. Then she grabbed a hold of my back right at the curve and began rocking me back and forth. As she did this, I felt intense cold, but her hands were red with heat. She continued rocking me, until I felt like a little baby lying on my back. You know how they lay with their legs up, playing with their toes. In that moment I *was* a baby. It felt so sweet and innocent, so joyful. Babies are so free, and I think we spend our whole lives trying to get back to that sense of freedom. As I lay there on the table feeling the joyful lightness of infancy, I couldn't help but be overwhelmed by that same freedom. The freedom to just be. How often do we actually allow ourselves this simple pleasure? I relished every moment of it. I felt playful, vulnerable, and a little regressed. I mean my toes were all the entertainment I required. Quite suddenly, in the midst of my reverie, Cheryl shoved her perfectly manicured fingers right into the soft spot just below my sternum. She went in so deeply, I think she could have wrapped those fingers right around my spine. And then I was sobbing, crying so hard with Cheryl's hand so deep in my gut that breathing became impractical; but I felt nothing but pure, unadulterated joy. I was one with everything. I was with Hohepa. I saw my father. I could feel other healers who had passed. Everyone in the world, every human being was like a best friend. I embraced them all with sincere gratitude. The flowers were with me, the trees were wonderful conversationalists, the birds sang out sweeter, the light shone brighter. It was a new day, a new dawn. It was timeless, potent, and rapturous. There really wasn't anything else to do but cry from the intense love I felt for everything.

Why did I keep repeating this experience? I had this same feeling after my class at the ashram. And it happened again in the cathedral at Santiago. And I had it in Ro-Hun sessions, in meditations, and even sitting at a gas station in Utah. This profound union with everything was occurring more and more frequently in my life, and I was becoming addicted to it. This was bliss. My awareness became so expanded that I no longer recognized good or bad, I just felt love and life was like a song. How could I keep this feeling going? Was there a possibility to make this the norm?

Looking back at all of the situations, I realized that the common denominator was surrender. It didn't matter if I had a healer there or if I was in a church or standing on a hilltop.

It wasn't about who was with me or where I was. It was about giving up a little self-importance and finding my place in the grand scheme of things. But guess where I found myself when I did this? Everywhere! I used to think my personality was important. In fact, it meant everything to be a certain way, with a certain outlook and certain convictions. How limiting that seems when you are experiencing boundlessness! Personalities are fun, and we can dress them up and have a good time, but in those moments I touched the truth: that I am infinite spirit experiencing a personality with all of its ups and downs. I can experience all kinds of states of being, but the highest and the truest state is the one where my awareness is trained to the infinite and no longer limited by my physical perceptions. We are all capable of living with this expanded awareness. It's all about surrender.

I try to practice surrendering in my daily life, in hopes that this training will bring me daily peace. Of course it isn't always easy for me to give up control. Sure, I can let my husband cook dinner, but many times I still have to shove a sock in my mouth to keep myself from calling out instructions from the living room: "Don't add any funky spices!" "No experimenting!"

In order to really give up control, I have to find that peaceful state, that broadened frame of mind within which I feel safe enough to truly allow the world to just be. Then I forget all about the outcome because when you feel boundless, who cares if the spaghetti sauce has a little more oregano in it then you might like. You found peace. Isn't that more important?

Before, I believed I had to control everything because of fear. If I didn't have a firm grip on every situation, I felt unsafe, reckless. Now that I have experienced that intoxicating bliss numerous times, I'm finding it easier to take a chance and let go. But the true test is always the hardest: searching for healing is also a form of control. I want my spine to improve, and I want it done when I want and how I want – preferably now and painlessly. This kind of release takes incredible trust or it takes a drastic situation where no other choice exists; like a near-death experience or a huge accident. People who have gone through these extreme experiences come back profoundly changed, but it is possible to shift without going through something so painful. It's as simple as a choice: learn to trust that all is well, and life gets a lot easier.

I worked regularly with Cheryl for over a year. We met in Lily Dale, in Wheeling, and in our home in Georgia. During this time, I started to receive comments from many quarters regarding children. I've always been nervous about having a baby. It is the big question mark floating just above the horizon, but it was always in the distance. Now, it seemed to be right in front of me. I had a reading from a friend who said she felt two babies around me who were eager to come through. Cheryl kept begging me to be careful, so that she could work a little longer before I got pregnant. One of my closest friends asked me if I was pregnant every time we spoke, saying she had a feeling it was going to happen soon. It was nice to see that everyone wanted us to have a family, but no one was answering my real question—sure I could get pregnant, but would I be okay carrying a baby?

Ask and you shall receive. After all of these comments, the idea of motherhood was very much on my mind. Then we went to Belgium to visit Brecht's family, and his mother sent me to an osteopath that she liked. Osteopathy in Europe is much like chiropractic here. They do adjustments, but many of them also do massage, myofascial release, and cranial-sacral therapy. This osteopath was also a bit of an eccentric, but I immediately liked him and his office.

The office was an old barn that had been refurbished, and like most things in Belgium, it was charming, understated, and very correct. The ceilings were high, but not intimidating. The walls were stark white, but the vintage wood of the doors, trim, and baseboards balanced this nicely. The floors were laid with warmly colored tile, and the furniture was charmingly mismatched. We were in the countryside, so out of every window was greenery, and the aging glass of the window panes slightly distorted the view, so one had the pleasing feeling that this office was somehow lost in time. He himself was somewhat disheveled with kind eyes and a welcoming manner. There was something about him, though. I always had the feeling he wasn't sharing with me the full spectrum of his perceptions.

"Australia," he said.

I was lying on his table, face up, and he had his hands on my hips checking the flexibility of my pelvis.

"Yes? What about it?"

"Something important is going to happen to you in Australia. It will unlock something for you. It will be the key to your healing."

"Well, I have no interest in Australia, and no plans to go there. If you had said New Zealand, then I'd understand."

He smiled and continued working. "It's right here in your pelvis."

"What is?"

"Australia."

"Australia is in my pelvis?" I asked, a little sarcastically.

"Sometimes, you can't see the path, but all of the choices you make lead you in one direction. You can't help but make these choices. It's who you are. Sometimes, someone can see a little further ahead than you can, and what I see is Australia. Whether you want it or not, you'll be there. And while you are there, you could conceive a child. So, if you don't think it's a good time, you should be very careful."

"Hm-m-m" was all I could think of to say.

He worked on my pelvis a little longer and then came to the head of the table. He put his hands just at the base of my skull, and I allowed the weight of my head to relax into them. A few seconds later, I felt the meditative state that I have learned to associate with cranial-sacral work come over me.

We finished the session, and as I was getting ready to leave he said, "You shouldn't worry about it, you know."

"Shouldn't worry about what?" I asked, distracted as I tried to find my wallet at the bottom of my purse.

"About children. You are going to have children, and there won't be any problem."

I stopped for a moment and stared at him. I hadn't mentioned anything about those fears.

"Thank you," I said. "I really appreciate that." I paid him and left to find Brecht and share the good news.

When I returned to the States, I again sought treatment with Cheryl; this time with the conviction that I was going to do everything I could to prepare my body for pregnancy. I can remember one day in particular we were in session and suddenly she began to twist me into all kinds of strange positions. This was not so special, since Cheryl is adept at winding the body into all manner of contortions. However, on this day it was like a dance. Cheryl all but disappeared, and I was there alone with my body. Before I knew it I was laughing, then crying, then laughing, then crying. I didn't know what was happening. I thought maybe I was going crazy, but I felt safe enough to relax and let go.

As the dance continued I became aware of a part of myself that I had never met before. It began to unfold within me. Deep inside, at the center of my being, I felt it unwinding. It stretched and twisted and unfolded as Cheryl moved me all around the table. On the outside it probably looked like total chaos, with Cheryl twisting and untwisting my arms and legs and me laughing and crying in more and more rapid successions. I had again attained that heightened awareness that reveals the beautiful nature of reality and that familiar feeling of overwhelming bliss. I was joyful and innocent, like a child. I was vulnerable, but strong. I was laughing and crying so hard because I was overjoyed to find my true self, and so overwhelmed at the sweetness of reconnection.

Six months later . . . .

8

Adrian

"Life is either a daring adventure or nothing."
—Helen Keller

I HAD THE EASIEST pregnancy anyone could ask for. No morning sickness, no back pain (remarkably), no big mood swings, only a few random days of swollen feet and a couple weeks of hip pain that went away after a few adjustments. I loved my big belly. I was proud of the way it popped out like a beach ball, big and strong. It was the quintessential pregnant belly.

I went into labor on my due date. My water broke at 10:30 P.M. while I was laying in bed reading. When I got up to use the bathroom for the tenth time, I suddenly felt a trickle of water, and then another.

"Honey, I think the baby is coming."

"Really? How do you know?"

"Well, there's water coming out of me."

"Oh! Well, what should we do?"

"I don't know! Should we call Jen?"

"Yes, definitely call Jen."

Jen was our midwife.

I continued my trip to the bathroom, this time with phone in hand, and dialed Jen. I told her the situation and asked her what I should do.

"Go back to bed and call me when it's too intense."

"That's it?" I asked.

"Yes, believe me. You need to conserve your energy for later."

"Okay, I'll call you when it gets 'too intense.'"

I hung up the phone. Knowing myself, I thought, the baby might already be here by the time I think it's too intense—I hate to be considered a wimp.

I sat up in bed and continued to read. Brecht dozed beside me, waking up occasionally to ask how I was doing.

Finally, around 2 A.M. the bed was no longer comfortable. We moved to the living room and sat on the floor. Brecht, of course, found us an appropriate soundtrack, and tonight it was Krishna Das. Every time a contraction came, I hugged Brecht around the neck and let myself sort of dangle. I breathed, crouched, sat on the exercise ball and did a fair share of moaning. I lost all track of time, but the music soothed me. The waves of pain felt like opportunities, moments when I could really let go and allow the pain to be there. There was no other choice. I had to go through it. In moments like this, it is best to surrender. I smiled at Brecht and tears streamed down my face.

"This is so spiritual," I cried. "I mean I really have to let go."

I hugged Brecht and kissed him. I was so happy and so excited for Adrian to arrive.

We decided at some point to fill the bathtub. I rested in there for a while, but as the contractions became more intense, I started shivering. I turned the water on hotter and hotter, but

I couldn't stop the shaking and the pains were coming more and more frequently. By this point it was about 5:30 A.M. We figured it was time to call Jen.

I was still in the tub when Jen arrived around 6 A.M. I had draped hot washcloths all over me, but the shivering was getting very annoying, and the pain wasn't feeling very spiritual anymore. Jen told me the shivering was from the shift in hormones. She measured me and said I was at 7.5 cm.

"What does that mean?" I asked. "How much longer?"

"Everyone's different, Sara; it could be another three or four hours."

I couldn't reply because another round of pain began. I gripped the sides of the tub and tried to breathe. Then I looked at the two of them, my husband and my midwife, having a little chit-chat on the bathroom floor while I writhed in pain and shivered away in the tub, and for a second the absurdity of the scene hit me. Here I was more uncomfortable than I had ever been in my life, in an endless hell, really, and right in front of me, like some sort of cosmic joke, was the chirpiest duo you ever did see, just laughing and chatting like it was Christmas Eve and Santa was on his way with a cuddly little baby just for them.

Well, that's how it *felt*, anyway!

Finally, the tub was too constricting, and we made preparations to hoist me out of the water, towel me down and wrap me in a robe. Then we moved to the kitchen. Soon after this, I noticed the quality of the contractions changed. It was time to push. Brecht sat behind me in a chair and I sat between his legs with my hands resting on his thighs. Every time a contraction came I clenched his hands with everything I had.

"Ahhh! Let me get my ring off first, Sara!"

I pushed and pushed, thinking it would never end. Then Jen said she could see Adrian's head. She invited Brecht to come around and have a look.

"No way!" I said.

"Stay where you are! I can't see him either, Brecht. Please, don't move!"

It was just a few more pushes after this and Adrian was there, screaming and healthy.

"He's perfect!" Brecht cried.

Jen wrapped him in a blanket and handed him to us. Our little boy was finally here.

Four months later, we decided a trip to Key West to see my chiropractor, Debbie, was in order. I could get a new X-ray so we could see how my spine faired during the pregnancy, and she could meet Adrian.

We arrived in Key West on a sunny October afternoon, and I phoned Debbie's office to make the appointment. I waited as the receptionist checked the book.

"You could come right now!"

"Oh, okay. Brecht, we can come right now." I said, feeling the dread mounting. I hate getting X-rays.

"I'm ready!"

"Okay," I said into the phone "we'll be right over."

I walked into Debbie's new office and surveyed the waiting room. There was a woman sitting alone on one side, but the other seats were empty. Brecht came in behind me carrying Adrian, and we all sat on a neatly cushioned bench flanked by piles of magazines. I flipped through one quickly and tossed it aside.

"Don't talk to me. I'm too nervous." I said.

Brecht played with his phone, and Adrian stared up at me, blinking, expectant. I smiled. Then Debbie's assistant came to take me to the X-ray room. She walked me down the hallway, lightly chatting, and I offered a couple noncommittal "mm-hm's." By the time we arrived at the dark, little room down the hall, I had managed to make myself almost calm. She immediately commenced to measuring and weighing me.

"I still have a long way to go before all of this baby weight is off."

I commented as I stared at myself in the mirror. She was busy taking some notes.

"Don't be too hard on yourself," she said as she scribbled.

When it was time, she positioned me in front of the film and told me to stand perfectly still with my mouth open wide.

"That's it." She said and walked behind the barrier so that I was standing alone staring down the machine. The familiar humming began, and ten seconds later it was all over. One more X-ray.

I went back to the main office and sank onto the bench next to Brecht. More people were in the waiting room now, and I felt the familiar pang of shame that they might see my X-rays and gasp. Worse than that was anticipating Brecht's reaction. He had never seen my X-rays. There he was sitting quietly beside me, so unsuspecting. I distractedly pulled on my lips, a nervous habit. Now my secret would be revealed. He would see how bad things really were. I was a liar for keeping it from him. I was putting our son at risk with my degenerate gene pool. I pictured my mother-in-law with a smug grin and imagined a condescending tone as she uttered that awful phrase: I told you so . . . .

Debbie's head appeared around the corner. The inevitable moment had arrived. We gathered in a treatment room down the hall and when she hung the film so the light shone through, I looked away because I didn't want to see his face. Brecht went right up to it. I could see him comparing the new and old images. I paced the room keeping my eyes on Adrian and trying to avoid a confrontation with the film. This was awkward because they were on opposite ends of the room, so my pacing was really a short step, a swivel and then another step and a swivel.

"I think it got better, Sara. These vertebrae are more level." He paused to keep studying.

"Let Debbie look at it." I said.

She peered at my spine, dissecting every angle; checking and double checking. Finally . . . .

"He's right, it is better. The rotation is better, L4 and L5 are sitting more level and the upper curve has held its own really well."

"This is great!" she went on. "Normally just staying the same makes me really happy, but yours improved!"

She did a little jig to show how happy she was, and for the first time, with my X-ray right in front of me, I felt like dancing too.

Part II

9

Willingness

"Knock, And He'll open the door
Vanish, And He'll make you shine like the sun
Fall, And He'll raise you to the heavens
Become nothing, And He'll turn you into everything."
—Rumi

LIFE IS LIKE A BLANKET we are weaving every day with our thoughts, our beliefs, and our choices. Every thread is another choice. As we live our daily lives, we create complex patterns from these choices. The overall direction of our lives is discernible in these patterns. When we pull on a thread, the whole pattern is affected. That thread could be anything from changing a long-standing belief to shifting our motivations and making a different choice. Whatever it is, the effects of that change influence the other areas of our lives. Thus, in healing, we must look to the entire picture, not just the disease. We must reevaluate everything about ourselves. We must become willing to experience the full breadth of the circumstances that have brought us into imbalance. And we must move forward with a sense of adventure, knowing that anything is possible. Miracles do happen, and they can happen to us.

How to do this?

Willingness to explore your self-imposed limitations is essential to growth and to healing, but you cannot simply decide to be willing. Everything is a journey and a process of unfoldment. You may be saying right now, "I *am* willing!" And what good does it do you? One part of you may be willing, but there are probably a lot of other parts that say "no way!" These could be fears of change or fears about taking risks or about other people's judgments. They could be subconscious fears to which you have no immediate access. Luckily, there is a way to access these faulty beliefs. You can use your life experiences to get you there. Every experience of disappointment or frustration is an opportunity to uncover your fears and insecurities. Thus, every experience is an opportunity to become willing because as you experience your own limitations and their impacts on your life, you naturally gain awareness. This little bit of enlightenment feels great, and when we experience it, we naturally want more: that's when we become willing. This may surprise you, but your life, the good and the bad, is perfectly constructed to benefit your spiritual evolution. The whole purpose of life is awakening, and you are designed for this purpose.

St. John of the Cross wrote about life as a chess game you play with God, who is teaching you how to play. The game is designed to suit your particular style of learning and to help you become a master of the game. In other words, your life circumstances are your opportunities for awakening. However, when we feel hurt or ashamed, we usually lash out or run from the experience rather than embracing it as an opportunity for growth. The world is in divine order. You will keep encountering these opportunities. The more resistant we are to these lessons, the more difficult the experiences will be until we finally give up a little control, until we finally say "enough is enough!" Then, we can change things. It's up to you how much you will endure until you reach this point.

And when you do, you can start exploring the beliefs you take for granted, the ones that you never thought to question. The vast majority of these beliefs cause suffering, but many of our ideas about life are so deeply ingrained in the collective psyche that they seem totally logical, even necessary to our survival. Many of us believe we need our anger, worry, and fear to survive. You may have such a deep-seated and firm conviction about something that it becomes extremely difficult to recognize how deeply it impacts the quality of your life.

We've all heard it said: everything happens for a reason. But what we rarely realize is that, most of the time, WE are the reason. We find ourselves in this or that situation because of choices we have made. These choices are the result of myriad beliefs we have about the world and ourselves. Put another way, you make choices based on your beliefs. Take a moment and consider what sorts of ideas you have about the world and your place in it. Do you have any negative ideas about how the world works? Do these negative ideas make you nervous, sad, angry, greedy, proud, or jealous? These are all forms of resistance. In the same way that love and humility can bring about a life of joy, resistance can bring about a life of discontent and strife. The most damning form of resistance is the one that keeps us from looking honestly at our fears, judgments, and compulsions.

Here is a very simple example. If you believe in the importance of being right, you will probably always make choices to ensure this. Your self-worth may be completely dependent on your need to be right (therefore you *resist* the possibility that you could sometimes be wrong). So, perhaps you will enter into intense discussions with everyone who has a different opinion than you or maybe you won't take big chances in life because you may fail. Perhaps you have abandoned someone in need because his life choices are different from yours. Whatever it is, this belief will determine the direction of your life. I have met people who are so insistent on being "taken seriously" that they live in constant conflict with everything. Keeping a job is difficult because there is always a "problem person" in the office who has a different perspective. Living in community is almost impossible for people like this because there is no room for compromise when one person requires constant recognition. These types often end up tense, stressed out, and emotionally isolated, and the people closest to them are either resentful, exhausted, or both. As the feelings of loved ones become apparent, the resistant person becomes even more enmeshed in their need for approval, and the problems just get bigger. It's not what they want, but they are creating it through their beliefs and their behavior.

Sometimes we harbor beliefs or opinions about ourselves that are so well hidden we are totally unaware of them. This does not mean they are not influencing us. In fact, unconscious influences have even more power over us. Sometime ago, I was riding down a desert highway in southern Utah. Brecht was at the wheel as usual. We were on a month-long journey through the American Southwest, and like everything we do together, this trip had become yet another opportunity for self-exploration and spiritual growth. On that particular day, as we whizzed through the jagged red landscape, I was deep in contemplation over a spiritual teaching I had just been reading about: that you should be in the world but not of it; that you should interact with others while remaining free from entanglement. I could not grasp this teaching at all. In a world filled with nothing but entangling relationships, it sounded callous to me. How could I love someone without getting just a little entangled? Don't we praise empathy above all other feelings? Isn't marriage—supposedly the most recognizable expression of love—the epitome of entanglement? I bet there isn't a divorcee out there who can't tell you something about entanglement. I'm fairly certain that most people, divorced or not, understand the dilemma. I think we all rather crave some amount of entanglement, and the ones who don't? Well, they just don't get it.

But I couldn't just leave it at that. I wanted a real answer, not a write off, and I wasn't coming to one. The problem, it seemed to me, was that I didn't know what I was supposed to avoid. What is an entanglement, exactly? The answer came: an entanglement is an attachment. But what is an attachment? An attachment is a need or a desire. But what do I desire? I desire love, acceptance, and security. But isn't that normal? Silence.

I went round and round with this for a while, until I couldn't take it anymore. I decided to give up the search and let the answer come to me (this is an effective method I've finally adopted after years of inadequate answers springing from intense mental struggle). It only took a few hours, and I had my answer. We were parked at the gas pump of a small, dingy gas station in the middle of nowhere. It was one of those stations next to a sign that says, "No gas for 300 miles." I was leaning on the car watching Brecht pump gas, when I was suddenly overcome with an intense pit in my stomach and an episode of violent nausea. Wondering what this was all about I decided, inexplicably, that the best thing to do was, not to run to the bathroom, but to go into a meditation. Clutching my stomach, I babbled something to Brecht and slipped back into the car. As I sat quietly, I became aware of a dreadful feeling of disgust for myself. It rose up out of the depths like bubbling tar: a slimy, dark energy oozing out of me. It was thieving and insatiable. It wanted endless praise, and acknowledgment. I allowed the feeling to come over me, and the reason for the disgust became clear. I realized that every interaction I had was a cry for acceptance and acknowledgment. I entered every conversation in victimhood looking to the other person to supply me with enough energy to fill the void I felt inside. Like a parasite, I went from person to person seeking more and more appreciation. Without this appreciation, I felt empty and worthless. I believed that I was nothing if others did not approve of me.

No one, except someone very sensitive, would notice this about me. In fact, I run from victimhood. I eulogize strength and independence to anyone with the patience to listen, but we always preach what we need to learn. Somewhere tucked away deep inside like a dirty little secret was the most extreme victim. I saw how this feeling of victimhood caused me to abuse everyone: I wanted to feel strong, and someone was going to get me there! I sucked energy from everyone in my need for acceptance. But it was never enough, because the acceptance had to come from me, not them. In short, I was completely entangled in every interaction because I entered them in a desperate search for security. It seemed to me, I had no appreciation or love for myself at all! On a higher level, I longed to awaken. I wanted to experience the truth that we are all connected. But trapped in this energy, I felt alone and filled with fear: fear of emptiness, fear of unworthiness, fear of judgment and fear of my own insignificance. Fear is binding. It traps you. It is the very opposite of freedom. Thus, in my interactions I was attempting to bind people to me so that I felt less alone. How entangling is that!

Become familiar with your beliefs about yourself and learn how it is that they influence you. What choices do you make as a result of them? How do they influence your well-being? How entangled are you by your fears, your relationships, your life in general? Remember the only firm conviction worth having is the determination to understand your own makeup. Learn how you have wired yourself, and determine to break free from the host of knee-jerk reactions we all refer to as a personality. My father once received a beautiful message in a meditation. He didn't make much of it at the time, but the significance of the simple instruction quickly became apparent:

Reveal yourself.

Then true healing can begin.

10

Trusting the Incorruptible
Power of Stillness

"In stillness the world is restored."
—Lao Tzu

"You don't need to leave your room.
Remain sitting at your table and listen.
Don't even listen, simply wait.
Don't even wait.
Be quite still and solitary.
The world will freely offer itself up to you.
To be unmasked, it has no choice.
It will roll in ecstasy at your feet."
—Franz Kafka

AND HERE'S WHY. Our bodies, like our world, reflect our internal dynamics. If we have chaos within our consciousness, we have chaos within our bodies. We must clear out the fear and the junk we've carried around for years and learn again what it is to simply *be*. Get unfettered. Get guileless. Isn't that what our bodies are always telling us? We have forgotten how to listen to them. We don't realize that all of our emotional junk gets stored within them. We create our bodies every day with our thoughts and our beliefs. We treat a body like a machine: give it this, then do that, and everything will be fine. Unfortunately, some of the most devoted health nuts I know have some of the most persistent health problems.

So, there is something else going on. A body is like a child. We mold it with our perceptions, our misconceptions, our anger, fear, and grief. We also heal it with our joy, love, and gratitude. You know the expression, "Do as I say, not as I do?" Your body does what you do. Just like everything else in the physical world, your body reflects back to you what you are thinking and feeling. For a long time, my thoughts about my body were characterized by fear and anger. Through the years, I've tried to develop enough trust to transmute this fear into inspired action. Then again, I don't want to act to avoid suffering. I want to act to create joy and health. I want to relax into the knowing that I am safe and all is well.

But how can you let go and be joyful when you have no trust in a positive outcome? I recently found a journal entry I wrote a few months ago. I was lamenting my condition and feeling frustrated that I was not fully healed yet:

My happiness depends on the state of my back right now, but my back isn't going to change overnight; whereas, my happiness can change in an instant. Then again, I feel afraid of happiness because it feels like irresponsibility: I'll be so happy that I'll forget all about my back and then it will get really bad. I have held onto the belief that my worry is what keeps me on the healing path. If I worry about it, I focus on it, and that means I work to improve it.

Can I be happy and work on improving it? Somehow this question makes me feel empty. Like working on it in happiness is a waste of time.

Even more than that, it seems to me that I believe it only makes sense to try and heal my back if I'm miserable about it. If I'm not miserable what needs to change? Isn't all action about avoiding misery? So, does this mean I should just stay miserable until I'm healed?

Is avoiding worry and misery really my only motivator? Can I live safely without all of this suffering?

As I read these words, I wondered, are these negative motivators only affecting my search for healing? How much of my daily activity is about "avoiding misery" rather than creating joy? If I used misery to motivate my healing work, I must be using it to create other areas of my life too. I suspected that even in moments when I felt I was acting from joy, these actions were also intended to distract me from anxiety, fear, and worry. A habit is a habit, and this seemed like an overarching pattern in my life. If that was true, I was determined to recognize it. After all, if I believed that everything in life is connected, then I had to admit that compulsively avoiding suffering on one level was limiting my progress on other levels. Wasn't it my goal to transcend these limitations and attain true and total healing?

For days after reading this, I observed my motivations. I pondered the notion of stillness. I sat on the couch and refused to move until I felt that the impulse was not coming from a need to distract myself. I sat through anxiety. I sat through stress that things weren't getting done. I sat through Brecht's wary glances as he went about his daily chores. Laundry was piling up. The house was getting very dirty, and I was getting very bored. I felt totally apathetic and completely at a loss. What was I waiting for? What part of me was I trying to contact? Then I remembered a seminar I attended years ago. The teacher gave us a technique to reach our divine center. You had to sit quietly and allow these negative emotions to well up within you. As each emotion reached its peak you imagined yourself falling through it to the next layer. Then you allowed this emotion to grow in intensity until it was almost unbearable, and again, you were told to fall into the next layer. I did this obediently through several layers and then I reached a place of total chaos. I couldn't focus on anything long enough to describe it. I couldn't relax enough to "fall through" like they wanted me to. It was just like being on a rollercoaster: up, down, up, down. I didn't think I could make it, but sometimes grace takes over and against all odds, we find the courage to trust. Eventually, somehow, I fell through that chaos and unfolded into a powerful and potent darkness. It was a vibrant universe, an ever-expanding source of energy and potential, an unfathomable and joyful dance, and it was me! Thinking back on that moment of revelation, I decided that I wanted my choices to be motivated by this part of me, not the fearful and timid part that was always looking for the safest, most secure solution. I wanted to experience this endless joy on a daily basis.

We human beings are bursting with powerful potential. We are filled with an unremitting joy. Unfortunately, we've mostly lost touch with this part of ourselves, and achieving joy is now synonymous with the bland and deadening notion of avoiding suffering. If we sit still for too long, we experience the judgments, fears, and worries that I experienced both at the seminar years ago and in my house during those three days of inactivity. The most common solution to deal with these feelings is to go, go, go. Distraction has become a way of life, and over the years we have created grander and grander methods of distraction. Yet, there doesn't seem to be a correlation between our level of distraction and our ability to maintain a peaceful and joyful existence.

In the name of being happy, we have become a society of doers. We have even turned the state of "being" into a process by endlessly creating and recreating our self-image. Who are you? You can communicate that to everyone through fashion, music, Facebook, Twitter, Pinterest, and probably some others I haven't heard of yet. Even the quest for relaxation is a form of doing. People *play* golf or *get* a massage or *watch* TV or *read* a book.

All of this doing leads to very little *being*. Our minds never receive the training required to bring peace to our lives so that we can simply be. So, when we are not distracted with our daily occupations, our minds are left fumbling, not knowing what to do. Anyway, I know mine is. The point is that if we don't train ourselves to enjoy stillness, we begin creating situations just to avoid the quiet, to *distract* ourselves from the quiet. Maybe we're workaholics or shopaholics or alcoholics or runners or cyclists or drama queens. Have you ever seen these people who always have something dramatic occurring? They are totally focused outward, never finding the time to be still and go within. Maybe we constantly have music playing or the TV on "just for some background noise." It really doesn't matter what the distraction is. The point is that precious few of us have frequent moments of total stillness. And this is a shame, because stillness is essential not only to a pleasant existence; it is essential to healing. Healing is always a return to your divine nature, to your true self. Eckhart Tolle tells us: "Your innermost sense of self, of who you are, is inseparable from stillness. This is the I Am that is deeper than name and form." How can we reach this powerful stillness within? We must pass through the fear, the worries, and the judgments to arrive there. We must face ourselves in the quiet moments, recognize the signs of imbalance, and start digging.

I used to believe that there was always something to worry about because every time I sat quietly with nothing to do, I worried. I grew anxious or judgmental, and all of my fears started showing themselves. Then it occurred to me: maybe this fear is what I'm avoiding when I'm running around "getting things done" or "enjoying my free time." Maybe these little nagging thoughts are unfinished business. Maybe I can learn something valuable about myself if I just begin to observe this pattern, instead of getting bogged down in the actual emotion. Worrying doesn't help anyway, and it certainly doesn't feel good. And no one ever said it was necessary, and even if they did, who's to say they were right?

I am convinced that if you trained yourself to be joyfully unoccupied, you might find that what you chose to occupy yourself with later would be very different because it wouldn't be driven by a compulsion to avoid stress and worry. Right now, every day is a race to stay just ahead of the scary emotions. We tell ourselves that we stay so active because otherwise life would be boring or unproductive. But most of our activities only bring us further from ourselves. Instead of distracting myself all of the time, I want to fuel my actions from the wisdom within me. I want to live my life with a deep sense of trust, knowing that everything is as it should be. I want to know that at every moment, with every action I am creating a joyful, healthy, and prosperous existence. I want the "do, do, do" part of me to be fueled by the stillness, the "I AM" that lives at the center of me. The only way I have found to do this is to lessen the amount of distraction in my life and to become inquisitive about my thoughts and choices. That way, when my "self" bubbles up from the depths, I will be present enough to listen.

Like I said: healing is revealing.

11

Receptivity and Honoring the Feminine: The Power of the Void

MOST OF US HAVE heard about male and female energy, and how we all have a bit of both within us. In truth, these energies are one, inseparable and incapable of existence as singular entities. However, in order to better understand the nature of the self, the functions of our creative life force are characterized along masculine and feminine lines. In Chinese medicine these energies are referred to as yin and yang. In Ayurveda, they are associated with Ida and Pingala. In the West we call it male and female. Whatever the name, the energy is the same. Male energy is of the day. It is associated with light, activity, and manifestation. It is the part of us that is constantly seeking expansion in the outer world (do, do, do!). We are all very familiar with this energy because our culture glorifies these traits, but what about the feminine energy? The yin aspect of self is associated with night or darkness, inner potency, pre-manifestation, introversion, and receptivity (stillness!). These qualities are also necessary for survival. The female energy is not so well understood; yet, it is still functioning to influence our lives.

The feminine energy is the stillness in our lives, the central core that is bursting with potential. Stillness is powerful because it is the precursor to creation. It is the point of greatest intensity before the bursting forth of new life. The feminine energy is not the "weak energy." It is the powerhouse of energy that brings us to the threshold of creative thought and manifestation. Feminine energy is the seed, bursting with life and potential, yet not fully manifested as the plant. It has all of the intelligence of life and creation. It sits quietly and waits for the correct environment, and once that seed bursts open, it is the male energy that spreads out into the world.

Feminine energy doesn't have to *do* anything. It simply is. There is no outward action associated with this energy. It is about being. Instead of this energy going out to meet the world, the world rises to meet it, which is why it is associated with receptivity. Yet, it is not passive; it is open. We have learned to associate receptivity and stillness with passivity and laziness, but true feminine energy is like a powerful vortex into which you are irresistibly and joyfully drawn. In its stillness it is potent. It draws you in.

Society *as a whole* (each and every one of us) has attempted to close this powerhouse of energy through the oppression of the feminine in all forms, but it is still at work in our lives. Although we are unaware of it, we still draw things to us. Although we do it unconsciously, we still create the quality of our lives. We believe we do this through constant striving and struggling to reach our goals, and, of course, we do achieve things through action. However, there is another force at work, and this force also determines the quality of our lives. If we were to become conscious of this powerful storehouse within us, we would never be the same again. We would be unstoppable, but more importantly, we would be whole.

This powerhouse is the feminine energy. Imagine being able to call to you everything that you need in life. I'm not talking about financial wealth and power over people. Power isn't synonymous with control. Money isn't synonymous with joy. I'm talking about seeing beyond the current equations. I'm talking about living beyond the structures provided for you. I'm talking about creating your heaven right here on Earth, about living a joyful life of self-empowerment. If you begin to explore the feminine energy, your current definition of self will begin to deteriorate. An entirely new way of life will unfold. That way of life is not pre-determined. It cannot be defined in terms of economics, politics, or personal style. It is truly original. It is not a leader and it is not a follower. It transcends these roles. There is no need to follow when you are at the center of creation. There is no need to lead, when your very existence is an expression of what is possible for everyone. People will not fear you. If they revere you, it will not matter because you will have no need for approval.

You can live your life exactly the way you want, but you must look inward. You must uncover all of the blocks that you have put up against your own powerful potential. Human beings are beautiful, loving, *powerful,* creatures, but we have ignored our own power. We bought into the story that the material world is more important than anything. We have abandoned ourselves in the name of "progress," "economic growth," "wealth," and "national pride." Keeping up with the Jones' is the top priority. Even a vacation can be a statement about who we are, how much money we make, and who we know. No one has truly benefited from this way of life. Very few people are experiencing everlasting joy and peace.

So many things in our world that are meant to improve us actually bring us further from our highest potential. These moral standards, familial obligations, work ethics, and individual styles are accepted as guiding principles towards becoming a good person, but they are superfluous. It's like asking a sheep dog to round up sheep that are already safe within the confines of a fence. They keep your behavior within a set boundary, but it's completely unnecessary. You are already infinitely wise and powerful. Wake up to your own *incorruptible* power. The solution isn't to wage war, it is to simply remove yourself from that equation. But you don't have to quit your job or move into an ashram. You just have to set the intention to begin living a little more consciously. Right now, living consciously may mean living sustainably, recycling, getting enough exercise, supporting local causes, etc. Those are all nice ways to spend your time, but they are conscientious decisions. They may help you feel better about yourself, but they don't bring you any closer to your true nature. They have nothing to do with consciousness. What I want is for all of us to *wake up*. Begin expressing our own divine nature.

The divine self isn't the province of religious leaders, governments, or corporate share-holders. You have the right to consciously access your own powerful vortex of feminine energy, and it will help you to be a fully functioning human being. This energy is incorruptible. When we are awake (that is, living consciously), human beings do little harm, because they are no longer guided by external principles of survival and competition or by the morals of the day. They do not need guidance because they have accessed the infinite intelligence that is the birthright of each and every one of us.

You may not know it, but you are already fully engaged with this infinite intelligence. You are already drawing things to you in a powerful and unstoppable way. This energy cannot be shut off, but as you are unaware of it, you mostly create chaos from it. Since you have been distracted from your internal environment for so long, you have no idea what it feels like. You don't know how to recognize a person who is on their way to this sort of life. They may even seem selfish to you. They may seem awkward or weird because they are not bound by the same externally derived principles that you are bound by. They are humble, but they are self-determined. They are wise and understanding, but they do not engage in your struggle. They laugh with you when you are sad, and they cry tears of joy when you are happy. They are peaceful—totally at ease—but they radiate charisma and power. They are fully engaged with their surroundings, yet they remain unattached. They are not needy. They love you, but they do not depend on you. They are raucous and wild, but they are not destructive, just joyful. They are spontaneous, without chaos, being beyond the illusory grasp of linear time. They are awake.

But aside from attending seminars to experience this powerful part of us, how can we cultivate such a spontaneous and joyful existence? In the face of all of our fears, how can we find the courage to trust that we are capable of attracting the things we want in life—the joy, the healing, the love? How can we use this powerful center to motivate and guide our actions? Divinely inspired action is spontaneous and wise, but can we learn this behavior or must we fall into it through the grace of God? I think both are possible, and as I look back on my life I see that I have already experienced profound healings and unbelievable strokes of luck without forethought and without planning. Perhaps these experiences were the result of a momentarily unfettered divine will working within me. I know I want more of these experiences, and the best method I can think of is to clear-cut a path through an overly cluttered consciousness and allow some of that divinity to shine through.

12

Listen

What does it all come down to? It's very simple, really. I have tried to cultivate a habit of listening: listening to my body, listening to myself, listening to others. The more I listen, the more I understand. The more I understand, the safer I feel to surrender my most sacred beliefs, my most prized justifications. As I give up these strongholds, I feel lighter, freer, and more capable of living successfully, healthfully, and joyfully.

I remind myself daily that I will listen more carefully and hear a lot more when the TV is off, when the Internet is down, and when I put aside my to-do list, even if it's just for a moment. I'm not saying I live in total peace—I have a six-month-old baby! But I try to create as much stillness in my world as I can, so that I can open up to the true stillness, the divine state that is my true self. This stillness has nothing to do with my physical activity. It is the nature of existence: if everything is boundless and infinite, there is nowhere to go; there is nothing to do. You are already there. You are already being.

In the brief moments when I can experience this powerful and enlightened state of awareness, I am in bliss. I know that I am a powerhouse of divine energy. I know that I am one with everything, that the world is like a playground, and that every one of us is a child just bursting with the desire to express every feeling, to create every moment with infinite joy . . . and to share this joyful love dance with everyone we meet. And when the light flickers and dims and I'm back in my living room or in my bed, I think of this wonderful journey and I pray that these moments come faster and faster. I can't wait to always feel free. I'm so proud to be human.

Epilogue

While writing this book, I have often chastised myself because I have yet to fully recover from scoliosis. Yes, I am doing better than I was. I have very little pain, just occasional soreness and mild discomfort. Yoga takes care of most of it. My body is still in good alignment, as if the rest of me has found symmetry, even if my spine has not. All in all, I am able to manage a pretty severe curve with little to no trouble. I continue to meet with Cheryl, and I know that she will help me to create even more balance. But I haven't fully healed. It's easy, sometimes, to look at myself and think "fraud, failure." I have been plagued by insecurities and the fear that many will disregard my story because there is not complete physical healing; but I have pushed on because the message was always transforming. I know now that this is a book about finding peace of mind and happiness no matter what the circumstance. My particular circumstance, the thing I have often blamed for all of my problems, is scoliosis. Maybe yours is something different. Whatever it is, I say use it to grow. Let your struggle, if you have one, be for spiritual understanding. Let it be for awakening. My search for healing has enlivened me. It has blessed me with a hunger for revelation: the uncovering of the sacred within me.

When I was younger I thought of boundaries as borders, lines I could not cross. We all live within a set of boundaries: the boundaries of our hometowns, the boundaries of our families, our homes, our beliefs, and most pervasive of all, our bodies. For me, happiness was an impregnable fortress guarded on all sides by scoliosis. I felt inhibited and trapped, forever doomed to miss my chance at happiness because of this deformity. Scoliosis was the ultimate un-crossable border. But happiness doesn't come because we fulfilled a set of circumstances. True joy is the result of surrender: that means no requirements, and if we ever have the courage to drop our prerequisites for happiness, we will come to know the truth. The truth is that within every boundary there exists an infinite amount of choices and possibilities, and no matter how tightly we constrict our lives, we are boundless. Our thoughts and belief systems might bring us into the tiniest jail cell, literally or metaphorically, but the door is always open. We are always free.

My story isn't over yet, and neither is yours. Every day can be an adventure in self-discovery. Always remember, joy comes from within. So, reveal, reveal, reveal. If you promise yourself to act consciously, to uncover the belief systems that so often push us into anger, worry and doubt, then you will begin to transform because it doesn't matter what is happening in your environment – and that includes your body. You can be blissful and imperfect. So, don't put conditions on your happiness. This is your moment, right now. Enjoy it.

About the Author

 Sara Chetkin graduated from Skidmore College in 2001 with a Bachelor of Arts in Anthropology. In 2007 she earned a Master of Science in Acupuncture and Oriental medicine from the New England School of Acupuncture. She is a Ro-Hun therapist and an ordained minister with the Church of Wisdom, Delphi University. She lives in New York with her husband, Brecht, and their son, Adrian.

Related Titles

If you enjoyed *The Healing Curve,* you may also enjoy other Rainbow Ridge titles. Read more about them at *www.rainbowridgebooks.com.*

The Divine Mother Speaks: The Healing of the Human Heart
by Rashmi Khilnani

The Buddha Speaks: To the Buddha Nature Within
by Rashmi Khilnani

The Cosmic Internet: Explanations from the Other Side
by Frank DeMarco

Conversations with Jesus: An Intimate Journey
by Alexis Eldridge

Conversations with Jesus, Book 2: An Invitation to Dance
by Alexis Eldridge

Dialogue with the Devil: Enlightenment for the Unwilling
by Yves Patak

Dance of the Electric Hummingbird
by Patricia Walker

Coming Full Circle: Ancient Teachings for a Modern World
by Lynn Andrews

Afterlife Conversations with Hemingway: A Dialogue on
His Life, His Work and the Myth
by Frank DeMarco

Consciousness: Bridging the Gap Between Conventional Science
and the New Super Science of Quantum Mechanics
by Eva Herr

Jesusgate: A History of Concealment Unraveled
by Ernie Bringas

Messiah's Handbook: Reminders for the Advanced Soul
by Richard Bach

Blue Sky, White Clouds
by Eliezer Sobel

Inner Vegas: Creating Miracles, Abundance, and Health
by Joe Gallenberger

Flames and Smoke Visible
by Danny Lliteras

What To Do When You're Dead
by Sondra Sneed